The Spider
Principle

The Spider Principle

How to Tailor Your Marketing Network to Suit Local Needs

IAN LINTON

FINANCIAL TIMES

PITMAN PUBLISHING

PITMAN PUBLISHING
128 Long Acre, London WC2E 9AN

A Division of Longman Group UK Limited

© Ian Linton, 1993

First published in Great Britain 1993

British Library cataloguing in Publication Data
A CIP catalogue record for this book can be obtained from the British Library.

ISBN 0 273 60328 0

Phototypeset in Linotron Times Roman
by Northern Phototypesetting Co. Ltd., Bolton
Printed and bound in Great Britain by
Biddles Ltd., Guildford and King's Lynn

CONTENTS

Recognition programmes – Simple programme
administration – Presenting to the local management team

National research – Local research – Success factors –
Assessing the distributor profile – Local focus groups – Key
differentiators – Developing a support package – Assessing
promotional impact

Overall objectives – SWOT analysis – Identifying key
market sectors – Competitive activity – Market sector
activities – Customer focus standards – Customer
satisfaction objectives – Developing skills – Salesforce
actions – Generating enquiries – Customer incentives –
Customer loyalty actions – Advertising – Direct mail –
Special campaigns – Joint promotions – Wholesale activities
– Sales incentive programmes – Using new technology –
Perceived position – Review process

Setting overall objectives – Assessing strengths and
weaknesses – Dealing with competitive activity – Supporting
market sector activities – Ensuring customer focus –
Improving customer satisfaction – Developing skills –
Improving salesforce performance – Generating enquiries –
Offering customer incentives – Improving customer loyalty
– Making the best use of advertising – Supporting direct
marketing – Helping local outlets to run special campaigns –
Running joint promotions – Developing wholesale activities
– Operating sales incentives – Introducing new technology –
Internal resources – Responding to a local marketing plan

National support programmes – Building network identity –
Strategic promotions – Imposing corporate identity –

OVERVIEW OF THE BOOK

BUILDING LOCAL BUSINESSES

This chapter explains the reasons why local outlets are important and outlines the benefits to companies supplying both products and services. It explains why local outlets should be treated as independent small businesses, rather than outposts of head office, and analyses the strengths and weaknesses of the approach. It then looks in more detail at specific opportunities and problems in applying the principle of independent businesses to branch offices and independent multiple franchise outlets. The chapter then considers the success factors that can be used to measure the potential of a local outlet as an independent business. Finally, it shows how traditional support policies go only part of the way to meeting the criteria for developing successful local businesses.

AGENDA FOR LOCAL MARKETING

This chapter is structured as an agenda to help you review the current status of your local network and set objectives for improving performance. The first part helps you evaluate the importance of local markets to your organisation and asks you to consider whether your local network will continue to meet your changing needs. The section, 'Scope of network plans', looks at the geographical context of networks and asks you to consider whether you have the resources to support your plans. By analysing the current status of your network, you can focus on the right priorities, rather than heading in the wrong direction. The section, 'Reasons for action', provides a number of scenarios to help you identify your most important development tasks. The next section recommends turning those tasks into quantifiable activities by measuring current performance and setting specific targets. The section on operating constraints asks you to consider whether you need to strengthen the degree of control over your local outlets before implementing improvement plans. You must also assess the likely impact of competitive activity on your plans. By assessing your current support programmes, you will be able to identify additional support requirements and quantify the resources you need to provide support. The chapter recommends that you establish support priorities and a timetable for change. Finally, the chapter asks you to state the planned perception for your local network – how you want customers to view it.

FOCUSING ON THE NEEDS OF LOCAL OUTLETS

This chapter helps you to look at marketing support programmes from the point of view of the outlets – what do *they* want from the relationship with the supplier? Products that offer broad market coverage and fast-moving products will help them to build their business. To sell your products professionally, they need comprehensive product information. A clear statement of corporate direction, together with regular, up-to-date information on company developments, will ensure that local outlets understand your business and can plan change in their business to meet your changing requirements. The chapter stresses the importance of regular contact with local outlets and shows how technical support and comprehensive training and development programmes will help them improve the performance of their business in partnership with you. Local outlets expect you to provide effective national marketing support to build their business and they want the means to provide their own local input to marketing programmes. The chapter outlines the different types of support that help the local outlet to build its business – traffic-building programmes, customer loyalty programmes, sales incentives and recognition programmes. Most importantly, it shows how marketing programmes should be easy to use and simple to administer. Finally, the chapter outlines different options for presenting the support programme to a local management team as part of a continuing relationship or to attract new outlets.

ASSESSING MARKET OPPORTUNITIES

This chapter outlines the type of research that should be carried out as a basis for planning local support programmes. It explains how local outlets are in the best position to understand their customers and their local markets, but local research must be integrated with information from national research programmes. The chapter describes how suppliers can provide their local outlets with suitable data and help them carry out their research in a professional way. Research helps both parties to determine the success factors for local marketing and provides a basis for assessing the distributor profile and identifying the key differentiators that need to be addressed in developing a support package. The chapter shows how test marketing, pilot programmes and promotional-response tracking can be used to evaluate the potential impact of different marketing strategies.

DEVELOPING A LOCAL MARKETING PLAN

This chapter provides the basis for a local marketing plan that is prepared jointly by the local outlet and the supplier. It goes through each stage of the planning process to show the factors the local outlet should consider. The chapter divides the plan into the following areas: overall objectives, SWOT analysis, identifying key market sectors, competitive activity, market sector activities, customer focus standards, customer satisfaction objectives, developing skills, salesforce actions, generating enquiries, customer incentives, customer loyalty actions, advertising, direct mail, special campaigns, joint promotions, wholesale activities, sales incentive programmes, using new technology, and perceived position. For each factor, the chapter provides a list of actions that might be taken by a fictitious car dealership. Finally, the chapter suggests a review process to ensure that the plan is acceptable to both parties.

ASSESSING SUPPORT REQUIREMENTS

This chapter shows how information from the local marketing plan can be used to develop a local support strategy. It reviews the support options available against each of the categories in the marketing plan and shows how to select the right option for different situations. It covers the following topics: setting overall objectives, assessing strengths and weaknesses, dealing with competitive activity, supporting market sector activities, ensuring customer focus, improving customer satisfaction, developing skills, improving salesforce performance, generating enquiries, offering customer incentives, improving customer loyalty, making the best use of advertising, supporting direct marketing, helping local outlets to run special campaigns, running joint promotions, developing wholesale activities, operating sales incentives and introducing new technology. The chapter also describes the internal resources needed to provide different levels of support and provides an example of a supplier's response to a local marketing plan.

TAILORING MARKETING PROGRAMMES

This chapter takes the support process a stage further by reviewing some of the techniques for tailoring support programmes to local market conditions. It shows that national support programmes are important in certain circumstances – building network identity, operating strategic promotions, achieving customer satisfaction objectives or imposing corporate identity. As a result, some support programmes must be mandatory. However, local outlets have the flexibility to participate in other programmes, depending on their business objectives. Modular support programmes are a versatile method of meeting the requirements of different markets, while techniques such as direct marketing enable a local outlet to target individual customers. The chapter explains a number of methods for customising local communications and supporting the sector marketing activities identified in the local marketing plan. Local event management can also be used to allow local outlets to put on events for their customers, with the backing of professional organisation. The chapter also looks at methods of customising local advertising, outlining funding options and providing guidelines for advertising in test markets and developing regional advertising programmes.

ACHIEVING CONSISTENT STANDARDS

This chapter describes one of the major problems faced by companies marketing through multiple outlets – how to ensure that customers receive the same standard of service in every branch. It shows how consistency can be used as the basis for branding local outlets in the same way as products. The chapter describes how quality standards such as BS 5750 are increasingly used at local level to measure and monitor performance in line with agreed standards. Staff skills are a key element of consistent performance and the chapter shows how local skills profiles are used to develop targeted training programmes. It is essential to communicate the benefits of training to local management and staff and to offer them flexible training options. The chapter provides examples of this and shows how some organisations deal with the problem of performance scatter by concentrating resources in centres of excellence or by utilising best practice from around their networks. The second part of the chapter provides detailed guidelines on achieving consistent visual standards, explaining the scope of corporate identity programmes and showing how to plan, implement and maintain them to achieve high standards of visual consistency.

FOCUS ON CUSTOMER CARE

This chapter shows how high standards of customer care are essential to building customer satisfaction and loyalty at local level and looks at the different ways in which customer care can be delivered. Customer focus panels, for example, help suppliers and local outlets identify their customers' expectations and the chapter shows how these expectations can be used to develop customer focus standards which can contribute to consistent standards of customer care in every local outlet. The chapter describes a number of different customer care programmes and customer care training options. It also shows the importance of measuring customer satisfaction through customer surveys and how customer comments can be used to compile customer satisfaction guides. Finally, the chapter shows how incentive and recognition schemes can be used to motivate local staff to achieve increasingly higher standards of customer satisfaction.

IMPROVING SALES PERFORMANCE

This chapter looks at a number of ways of helping local outlets to build sales and improve relationships with their customers. It begins by looking at the critical area of launching new products and services, showing how comprehensive information and support at each stage of the launch can help to build understanding, commitment and a successful launch. The same principles can be applied to existing products and services and the chapter looks at different approaches to providing product and marketing information. It shows how to keep information up to date using new technology such as laptop computers and interactive video and explains how these tools can be used to improve the selling process to the customer. The chapter gives examples of different types of incentive programme and shows how they can be structured to meet different marketing objectives.

DEVELOPING A CONTACT STRATEGY

This chapter discusses the crucial role of communications in improving local marketing performance. It outlines important objectives for a communications programme that will build understanding and commitment to success. The chapter shows how communications can be used to motivate local staff by recognising achievement and provides an example of the way effective communications can help to improve standards of customer service. The chapter reinforces the importance of personal contact in national and international markets and shows how national conferences, regional business meetings and branch briefings provide contact options to meet different communications objectives. The chapter recommends the appointment of a distributor specialist to concentrate on the quality of communications with local outlets, and outlines the specialist's key responsibilities. Finally, the chapter describes a number of options for improving staff communications using advanced technology such as corporate television networks or traditional printed material.

WORKING IN PARTNERSHIP

This chapter explores the potential for improving business performance when suppliers and local outlets work in partnership. For example, a supplier can provide its own customers with nationwide resources of a consistently high standard, not just by appointing and supporting local outlets, but by working closely with them. This section looks at the contribution of both parties to the partnership and also shows how they can use the process to broaden the service they both offer. Partnership can also form the basis for joint ventures that enable both parties to win new business that might not have been feasible without close co-operation. Finally, the chapter looks at the way new communications technology is helping to build stronger business links between suppliers and local outlets.

CONTROLLING LOCAL SUPPORT PROGRAMMES

This chapter looks at the options for managing and controlling local marketing support. It looks briefly at different budgeting options and examines a number of different approaches to providing central marketing support. Local advertising and other marketing services can be handled centrally for greater efficiency and co-ordination, but the chapter balances this against the resource requirements. It considers the options for providing a branch literature service and explains how guidelines on the use of promotional literature can avoid wasted effort. The chapter looks at different methods of administering and reporting on marketing programmes, emphasising that the most effective administration is often the simplest. It shows how marketing standards can be used to impose consistently high standards on locally produced material and explains the procedure for selecting and using external support agencies.

INTRODUCTION

The Spider Principle recognises the growing importance of strong networks in local marketing. A company can have well-managed central operations, but as soon as it begins to deal with customers outside its direct control, it depends on the quality and strength of its links with a branch or distributor network. Like the spider's web, the marketing network can take many different forms but, in every case, it depends on effective control from the centre, and it is only as strong as its weakest point.

This book aims to eliminate any weaknesses in your local marketing performance by helping you to build stronger links around your network and strengthen the relationship between your company at the core of the network and each of the outlets in the network. Like the spider, you begin at the centre and build a finely balanced network that is held together by the strength of the individual elements.

Networks like this gain increasing importance as companies rely on distributors, agents, branches or retailers to market their products locally. If they do not have a large salesforce to sell direct to customers throughout the marketplace, they must ensure that staff who are outside their control can deliver the right level of service to their customers. The standard of service a customer receives in just one branch or retail outlet influences their view of the whole organisation. That is why companies like McDonalds ensure that every outlet, everywhere in the world, provides the same high standards.

The scale of networks is increasing as companies regard markets around the world as their local market. For example, in 1993, the year this book was written, Ford launched the Modeo, the first 'world car' to be sold in all territories. In the same year, British Airways ran its first global television commercial – nothing changed except the language.

But not everything is on a global scale. Just a few years earlier, British Rail had restored a national service to regional autonomy with the establishment of Network SouthEast, ScotRail and other regions. It took the process further with the revival of pre-grouping line names – the London Tilbury and Southend Line, The Great Eastern, The Chiltern Line. It was trying to rekindle the enthusiasm of staff and customers for their own local service. Brewers too had reversed the trends of decades with the revival of regional brands of beer. This was partly a recognition of the 'real ale' cause but it also showed an understanding of the importance of regional preferences.

The question is – which strategy is right for the company aiming to improve its local marketing performance? Does it try to succeed through the sheer weight of national or global branding, or does it attempt to reflect local preferences by developing independent local strategies or brands?

The Spider Principle will allow companies to follow any of those options, provided they build strong links from the centre. Strong links will ensure that every branch can provide a quality service to customers.

However, it is important not to confuse quality of service with the content of the service. A petrol company operating sites on the motorway network and in rural areas would not expect to offer the same range of services at each site, but its customers would still expect the same quality of service. The content of the service could vary from 24-hour opening, foodstore, motorist's shop, toilets and a service bay to limited opening hours and a small motorist's shop. But, provided the customer still sees the petrol station staff as welcoming and helpful, the standard of service is perceived as consistent.

This gives companies a great deal of flexibility in planning how best to support local outlets and this book will review the options that are available. Our contention is that local markets vary and a local network support policy must reflect those differences. At its most extreme, the contention is that local outlets should be treated as independent, small local businesses offering a unique service to their local market. This appears to run counter to the demands for corporate identity and corporate branding that insist that every outlet looks the same and offers the same promise, but we believe that the two needs can be balanced. Provided the quality of service is consistent, the content can vary enormously.

To help readers focus on opportunities in local marketing networks, this book includes an agenda for selecting the elements of local market support most appropriate to your business and your customers.

The book also looks at ways of planning and implementing the right support strategy. The first part of the book explains the importance of developing a customised local marketing strategy, and the second part provides detailed guidelines on planning and implementing a customised local marketing policy.

A key feature of the development of local marketing programmes is the importance of international markets. Traditionally, companies divided their sales and marketing activities into home and export, but increasing globalisation and the opportunities provided by the single market means that this simple division is no longer practicable. Local marketing does not refer to regional variations in a national market, it refers to every market in the world.

1

BUILDING LOCAL BUSINESSES

THE IMPORTANCE OF LOCAL OUTLETS

Vinoo Iyer's book, *'Managing and Motivating Your Agents and Distributors'*, also in the Pitman Financial Times series, has shown that distributors, agents, local branches and retail outlets play a vital role in the process of getting products and services from a manufacturer or service supplier to the final customer. Local marketing support is an integral part of that process, but its importance is often overlooked. Suppliers assume that it is sufficient to apply a single national support policy to every outlet in a network and leave the outlet to make the best of this. The assumption is that the outlets are simply smaller versions of head office and operate in exactly the same way. This denies the real benefit of using local outlets because the local outlets are the supplier's 'personal presence' in the local market and should be encouraged to develop their individual skills. There are a number of important benefits in this approach:

- local outlets can provide a cost-effective supplement to the supplier's direct salesforce;
- local outlets understand their local market and can identify changing requirements quickly;
- they are aware of local competitors and can take individual actions to deal with competitive threats;
- they can respond quickly and effectively to change in the local marketplace or to specific customer requirements;
- they can build close and personal working relationships with individual customers, essential in building and retaining long-term

business;

- they can use local knowledge to tailor products or services to the local market;
- they can build small effective teams to operate flexibly in the changing conditions of the local market.

Supplementing the supplier's direct sales force

Distributors or branches do not simply take orders or hold stock for local distribution, they should be actively involved in marketing the supplier's products or services.

In the financial services sector, for example, the role of the high-street bank or building society branch manager, for instance, has changed rapidly from stern custodian of the institution's interests to a marketing manager responsible for effective marketing of a broad range of products and services. With the banks' and building societies' increasing interest in non-core products such as insurance, pensions, financial advice and other financial services, local branch staff are helping to supplement the traditional direct salesforce of insurance and pension companies.

In the manufacturing sector, distributors have traditionally dealt with the smaller local customers while the manufacturer dealt directly with larger national accounts. But, with the growth of multi-site customers and an increasing emphasis on service and aftercare as a key marketing activity, the distributors now play a more important role in offering a consistent level of nationwide service. In the construction equipment market, for example, an effective distributor salesforce can ensure that each local site receives a high standard of service and contributes to overall turnover, while the manufacturer's salesforce concentrates on maintaining relationships with the customer's head office team and carrying out strategic development work. The distributor salesforce extends the manufacturer's reach into the local market and enables it to provide a nationwide service without investing in a larger national sales infrastructure.

Understanding local markets

Comprehensive marketing information is vital to effective decision making, and local outlets are in the best position to understand their local market, which may reflect different patterns from the national market. They know the customers and they know why prospects are dealing with competitors. Because they are in regular contact with the local market, they can identify changes in the marketplace and respond quickly in a way that manufacturers or head office cannot match. When a number of financial institutions moved into estate agency during the housing boom of the 1980s, they did not start building their local networks from scratch, they acquired groups of successful local estate agents and utilised their local knowledge to provide a strong local presence.

Awareness of local competition

A head-office marketing team can gain a sound understanding of national competition by carrying out continuous research and monitoring competition, but the local outlet can supplement that by monitoring local competitive activity – new competitors moving into the area, local promotional activity, pricing, and levels of support from the competitor's head office. This information can be used either to build up a national picture of competitive activity or to develop local strategies for countering competitive activity. By encouraging local outlets to carry out their own competitive research and supplying them with national information, suppliers can help local outlets develop their own competitive edge.

Responding quickly to change

Local outlets have the flexibility to change their policies and their levels of service quickly in response to changes in demand or in competitive activity. Head-office changes take time to work through the system with corporate decisions to be made, schedules to adjust and procedures to be amended. Local outlets arc dealing in smaller numbers and the decision-making process is shorter.

Using a simple example, if a new business park opened in a town it would be relatively straightforward for a local bank branch to increase the number of staff working on business banking, whereas it would be a major decision for a bank that concentrates on personal banking to set up a business sector.

Building close working relationships with customers

Effective relationships are the key to long-term customer satisfaction and loyalty, and personal contact is an essential ingredient in building those relationships. Suppliers do not have the resources to develop close relationships with every customer, so they depend on local outlets for individual contact. The more support the supplier can provide to local outlet to free them for personal service, the more effective the results. Computers that speed up and simplify administrative routines can help to free staff from 'back-office' duties to concentrate on customer contact and give them greater freedom to be proactive.

Banks, for example, have moved many of their staff out into the open area in front of the service counter, ensuring a much higher level of personal contact with customers and helping to build long-term relationships. When ICL changed the way it delivered customer service, taking the engineers out of the branches and into centres of excellence, branch managers were freed from the task of administering and monitoring standards of service. Instead, they were able to spend more time making proactive customer care visits which helped to build partnerships between ICL and clients throughout the country.

Tailoring products and services

Local outlets can use their local marketing knowledge to tailor product and service offerings to customers. Although they may not physically change products, local outlets determine the range they carry and the prices they charge. At international level, a distributor network may carry a range of products and services customised to each of the national markets.

Taking the motor industry as an example, car manufacturers are increasingly producing standard cars to take advantage of economies of scale and the strength of global marketing. The Ford Mondeo is the first example of a 'global car' available in all markets; before that international cars would have carried different names in national markets, as well as any other product differences. A Vauxhall Astra, as it is known in the UK, is an Opel Kadett in continental Europe. But the name change disguises a host of product changes at national level such as: engine specifications to meet national emission and fuel economy standards; safety features to meet national requirements; special requirements such as daytime lights in Scandinavian countries.

Within national markets, local outlets still have an opportunity to customise the products for local markets. A local car dealer may offer a limited edition 'special' which includes a range of fitted options and badging unique to that dealership. This enables dealers to compete effectively, not only with other manufacturers' dealerships, but other regional dealers within their own network.

Building effective local teams

Because they understand local customer requirements in terms of products and levels of service, local outlets can identify the combination of skills and resources needed to provide the right local service. Local outlets can take advantage of distance learning and retail training programmes that are increasingly focused on the needs of individual outlets. Training and business support can be tailored to build the right team and deliver the highest levels of customer satisfaction in each territory.

TREATING LOCAL OUTLETS AS INDEPENDENT BUSINESSES

Given that local outlets play such an important role in product and service marketing, should they be treated as local outlets of a large organisation or should they be treated as independent local businesses which are motivated to succeed in their own market? There is a growing trend to treat local outlets as independent businesses because they can make an effective contribution if they are allowed to develop in their own direction. A number of factors make this practicable:

- local outlets are often owned or managed by people with a personal stake in the business, who are therefore highly motivated to succeed, personally and financially;
- it is easier to build team spirit in small units than in large organisations and team spirit can be crucial to success;
- decision making is rapid, with smaller teams to consult, branches can quickly put programmes into effect and make important changes;
- small units can be responsive, both because of their personal knowledge of the market and because of their commitment;
- smaller units are prepared to take risks because the rewards are tangible and because they operate in an environment they understand at first hand.

Motivation

One of the main problems in launching and implementing any marketing or business programme is motivation. If managers and staff are not committed to a programme, they will not give it their full support. In a widespread branch network, it may be even more difficult to build commitment because a programme or instruction appears to come down from a remote head office and the benefits may not be obvious to local staff.

However, if the programme can be positioned as directly relevant to the success of the local business and if the staff and the management team are in a position to benefit directly from a successful implementation, the programme will be more acceptable. While small businesses generally are more motivated to succeed, the motivation process can also be managed through personal and financial incentive schemes, recognition and award programmes, and other activities that encourage real commitment.

Team spirit

When the government announced draft measures to reduce the number of separate police authorities in England and Wales, there was a swift response from the police at grass roots level. A policeman belongs to the 'Met' or to the Suffolk Constabulary, not to some larger anonymous body and this feeling of team spirit and belonging is important to the success of day-to-day operations. In the Introduction, we mentioned how British Rail was attempting to build local team spirit through the revival of pre-grouping names such as the Great Eastern or The Chiltern Line. Programmes like this recognise the value of team spirit and this can be vital in improving local marketing performance.

Many business and marketing programmes require the joint efforts of groups of people to succeed. Given the relatively small numbers in local branches and the closer working relationships, it is easier to build team spirit. For example, customer care and customer satisfaction programmes involve many different departments and it is easy to identify the key team building tasks within a small unit.

Rapid decision making

Small units cut the time needed to put a programme into action. If a supplier needs to improve its competitive position in a specific market, it can delegate the decision making to a regional or local team which can quickly make the decisions and implement actions that will achieve success. A good example of a combined effort in a local market is shown by the American components manufacturer, Johnson Controls. When one of its European subsidiaries opens a new plant, the subsidiary has the autonomy to plan and build the plant that is right for its market, but the local management team gets the full support of all the other European plants. A European project team is brought together for the planning and implementation stages to ensure that the new plant reflects the combined experience and expertise of all the other plants. The new plant reflects the best practice available within Johnson Europe and is able to develop its independence from a strong base.

If an important customer needs a completely new form of service and support, a manufacturer may not be able to respond rapidly, but a local outlet with the right backing from a supplier can quickly make the decisions and implement the changes. A Japanese machine tool manufacturer, with a local manufacturing plant in the UK, provides each of its plants with advanced manufacturing control systems. Each local plant can respond to individual customers' requirements and deliver finished machines much faster than competitors. The parent company could have approached the problem differently by offering fast delivery of a limited standard range from stock, but this would have given them less flexibility in local markets. Instead, it delegates the decision making on products to the local outlet and provides a highly responsive service.

Responsive

Local outlets, as the last section described, are inherently more flexible than larger organisations. The decisions are taken by small groups and the consequences of decisions are likely to have a smaller impact than they would in a large organisation. Treating local outlets as small businesses reflects the move towards decentralisation in large corporations and is the equivalent of setting up a series of separate profit centres within a group, each with its own autonomous operating structure. Local outlets are closer to their customers and can respond quickly to the changes in customer needs. Local outlets can act as the eyes and ears of a head office and ensure that a company is adapting to change effectively throughout a network.

Risk taking

The entrepreneurial spirit that is evident in small local teams can also encourage the right level of commercial risk taking. A management team that is close to its market can assess the risk quickly and will also recognise the potential upside from that business risk. Provided a local outlet is given the right level of backing from head office, it should be in a position to innovate and deal with change in the local market and succeed.

WEAKNESSES OF THE 'INDEPENDENT BUSINESS' APPROACH

The benefits of using a branch or distributor network to build independent local businesses are clear, but there are also inherent weaknesses in the system which need to be overcome by providing the right level of support:

- it can be difficult to control local outlets when they are developing their own direction;
- local outlets may not have the financial resources to develop their business beyond a certain level;
- there may be limits on growth potential because of lack of local skills and resources;
- it may be difficult to brand a local network when it is developing in different directions;
- there may be problems in replicating standards of service to ensure consistency throughout a network;
- the success of the business may depend on the continued availability of a few key individuals.

Control

While a policy of building independent local businesses may provide a supplier with flexibility, it may also result in a loss of control. The head office team needs to ensure that each branch is contributing to the achievement of overall corporate objectives and is meeting its targets. If each branch is pursuing individual objectives and targets, it could be difficult to measure comparative performance and to exert overall control on the network.

Financial resources

If the local outlet is to succeed as an independent small business, it must have adequate funding to finance day-to-day work in progress and expansion. If the business has only limited funds, it may not be able to implement some of the marketing actions that are needed for success. The head-office team then has to decide how to allocate its own support budget. If it is providing a uniform support programme to the entire network, it is comparatively easy to distribute funds evenly, but if each outlet is pursuing its own business and marketing programme, the decisions on budget allocation become more difficult.

Growth limitations

Financial resources are just one aspect of the potential of individual outlets to grow and develop. Each outlet is likely to have finite resources in terms of space, equipment, people and management, and, although any business can expand, there may be limitations. For example, if there is a shortage of key skills, the outlets will be able to deliver only a certain level of service and, as an independent business, its potential may be severely limited.

Branding

Branding is increasingly important in retail development as suppliers seek to establish a strong, clear identity for their local outlets. They want to know that their local outlets are perceived as first choice for quality products and high standards of service and that customers will enjoy a high level of satisfaction whenever they visit a branch. The aim is to encourage customers to select a retail outlet in the same way as they select a product – by recognising its brand values. In the building supplies sector, Jewson used television advertising to brand its network of retail outlets. A campaign like this would only succeed if each branch in the network was operating to consistently high standards. Poor service at any outlet can quickly dilute the benefits of the television advertising. A network of independent distributors each pursuing their own local objectives may also make it difficult to develop a set of core brand values for the entire network.

Replication

Closely related to branding is the question of consistency throughout a network. The supplier team wants to know that its customers will be able to enjoy the same standards of service wherever they go. This is particularly important when a branch network is serving a number of major customers who operate on multiple sites and who will be concerned with consistent standards on every site.

A major national service contract, for example, would be awarded, not to the supplier with the largest number of local outlets, but to the supplier that could demonstrate control and consistent quality across a network that gave reasonable national coverage. Inconsistent standards force the customer to spend more management time on controlling supplier performance and may ultimately affect the quality of the customer's own service. An increasing number of service organisations are now submitting their services to a form of independent quality assessment such as BS 5750 to demonstrate that they can achieve the right level of consistency.

Dependence on individuals

In a distributor or retail network where local outlets build a strong independent business, there may be problems of succession if key individuals are not available. In a network operating uniform policies throughout the country, it would be easy to task key staff from other branches to implement the same policies, but developing a service that is tailored to local conditions depends on considerable local knowledge and that may not be transferable.

Overcoming the weaknesses

The potential weakness in a system of independent local businesses should not act as a barrier to development, rather they should help suppliers to identify the type of support they need to provide to overcome any potential difficulties.

OPPORTUNITIES AND PROBLEMS WITH CORPORATE BRANCH NETWORKS

This chapter has dealt in general terms with opportunities and problems in developing local outlets. The comments could apply to franchised or independent distributors or agents, as well as organisations with multiple outlets. This section looks at the particular challenges facing organisations with a network of local branch offices that may not see themselves as having sales or marketing responsibilities. Traditionally, branch offices were regarded as an outpost of head office. Head office did the business – marketing was situated there, product development was based at head office and the branches were simply local outlets conveniently located near customers. Provided they were run efficiently, there was no real pressure to develop new business.

Banks and building societies, for example, were regulated in the way they operated and there was little competition between the two. It was sufficient to have a presence in the marketplace to be offering a service. But with the advent of new forms of competition, it is hard to distinguish the service offered by the two. They offer similar ranges of services and products, they compete for the same account customers, hoping to win customers for life, and they have both transformed their branches into aggressive marketing operations. The branch manager is as likely to have marketing qualifications as administrative experience and performance is judged on turnover and profit as much as efficient branch management.

This section looks at the changing role of local corporate branches; unlike distributors they have only recently been given a sales and marketing role and they must now operate in the same way as independent retail outlets, utilising the full range of retailing techniques.

Marketing a wider range of products

Many of the significant changes in this area can be found in the travel sector. Local branch performance is important to two parties – the travel companies that market their products through travel agencies and the organisation that owns the network of agencies. Although the aim of both parties is to improve turnover and profit through each branch, their priorities are different.

- The travel companies want to ensure that branches understand their products and their markets, actively sell their products, offer their products rather than those of competitors and administer the transactions with customers efficiently. If they succeed in getting that level of response from each branch, they will have an efficient local marketing operation for their products, supplementing their own direct sales efforts.
- The owners of the network want to ensure that they can offer their customers the widest range of products and the highest standards of service. They must win distribution rights from travel companies to build up their own product portfolio and they must ensure that individual portfolios do not create an imbalance in their overall service. In order to expand, the owners must take on a broader portfolio of services and they must provide an efficient positive service on each one.

Developing retail skills

The key change in performance comes from recognising that each branch is a retail outlet, not an administrative office. It is no longer sufficient to open the doors and wait for customers to come in. A travel agency, a bank or a building society, or any 'branch office' has the potential to be a sales outlet.

The biggest change over the past five or six years has been in the physical layout and appearance of the branch office. The traditional counter service, which was the only 'front' to the business, has been replaced by open-plan sales and reception areas which put the customer first. In the travel agency, the emphasis is on merchandising, good display of the products available and skilled staff who are able to advise and sell to customers as well as taking their orders. That means the managers and the staff within the travel agency must understand the importance of good display and effective customer reception. The same changes have taken place in the banks and building societies where there are now large open areas for customers to meet branch staff when they wish to hold discussions.

Any organisation that wants to realise the marketing potential of its branch network must first change the culture of the network before providing support services.

Development of sales offices

These physical and cultural changes in the local branch have been accompanied by a change in the responsibilities of staff from administration to sales. Technology has speeded up many of the routine administrative procedures and freed staff for customer-facing duties.

In the travel agency, for example, computerised travel information and reservation systems mean that the time-consuming tasks of locating flights, checking availability, calculating discounts, ordering tickets and making reservations can all be handled on screen in a very short period of time. The accounting and administration that support these operations – issuing tickets, billing customers, charging the travel and putting the transaction onto the company's accounting systems – had also been handled manually, but can now be handled on the same computer.

The computer not only cuts down the back-office duties, it also provides sales information that can be used to identify national opportunities. For example, customer information is readily available through the computer so that staff can provide an informed response to travel requests and can also identify previous buying patterns so that they can sell additional products and services such as car hire, hotels and onward travel when a customer orders a ticket.

The emphasis is changing from merely handling requests efficiently to delivering additional levels of customer satisfaction.

Actively selling

This change in methods of service and the increase in customer contact gives branch offices the opportunity to sell a greater range of products and services to their customers. By gaining a better understanding of customer needs, staff can offer them a tailored package.

For example the regular business traveller can be offered the extra services described in the previous section and can also be kept up to date with new offers and services as they become available. A good sales representative keeps customers informed about faster journeys, better facilities with different airlines or travel operators, better deals on car hire or hotels, or bonuses for frequent travel, and wins business through that. Compare the business opportunities that presents with a situation where the branch office simply processes the customer's order.

Banks and building societies have the same opportunities to sell an increasing range of products to people who can be regarded as customers for life. For example, customers who take out mortgages are now offered insurance services, mortgage protection policies, and house contents insurance. Customers with investment accounts are offered financial advice and guidance, as well as a wider range of investment schemes. Ordinary current account holders are offered pensions and a host of loan schemes tailored to different purposes. Although most of these products and services have been available through the banks and building societies or through other financial institutions, they have not been sold actively and part of the management team's task is to develop sales of these additional products.

Dealing with variations in branch patterns

Developing sales and improving marketing performance in a corporate branch network takes a high level of support and initiative from the head-office team.

When Speedwing Training, part of British Airways, was developing its customer service training package for travel agencies it assessed a number of variables at branch level to ensure that training could be tailored to individual needs. The thinking behind the approach was that individual branches may not have the skills and resources to develop an effective sales operation, so it was important to deal with them individually. A survey, which formed the basis of a training database, looked at each branch from a number of perspectives:

- size;
- location and market coverage;
- current skills and training record;
- management structure;
- customer profile.

The training organisation could develop tailored development programmes based on this information and the same information could also be used to plan other market development and support programmes.

Comparative size

Although it seems an obvious conclusion that larger branches can devote more resources to sales and marketing, the branch may not have the skills and resources to accomplish this. In looking at the size of the branch, consider the number of people who are involved in marketing and customer service, the number of customers the branch deals with and their comparative turnover.

- Is the branch dealing with a small number of large customers or can it increase its customer base? Larger branches have the space to display more products and to devote more space to customer service.
- If they are members of a larger organisation, they will have the opportunity to use the facilities of the rest of the group and the head office and this can give them the ability to handle larger corporate clients.
- Smaller branches may not have the physical resources, but they can compensate by offering a flexible personal service to customers.
- Smaller branches may depend on larger local branches for their immediate marketing support and management – for example, a sub-branch might have only administrative staff and management and marketing may be handled from a larger local office; there would be difficulties in converting this branch to retailing.

Location

In assessing the potential contribution of the branch to the overall success of marketing operations, look at the location of the branch. Is it in the centre of a major conurbation, the catchment area for the business community or is it simply a local outlet with no clearly defined characteristics? The Speedwing Training survey looked at the location of branches to examine the type of business they might handle.

- If a branch was in a prime retail area it would attract a good level of passing trade, which meant that merchandising, window displays and an attractive retail environment where people could browse would be important.
- Other branches that had lower passing trade depended on the quality of their telephone response and their ability to develop long-term relations with business customers where there was less emphasis on impulse purchasing and shopping around.

Location can also be a crucial factor in the overall success of the branch network. The Post Office recently reviewed its location policy as part of a wider programme of meeting customer needs effectively. Many of its main sites were in traditional high-street shopping areas, but the older branches did not have the potential to take advantage of new counter technology or to set up retail centres. In considering relocation, they looked at entirely new sites within out-of-town shopping centres or in town centre shopping malls and, for their high-street sites, they considered locations within large retail outlets, provided they met the Post Office criteria for convenience, opening hours and ability to provide the right level of service.

The point about these moves is that the Post Office realised that it was a retailer as much as a provider of services, and it was essential that its own developments were in line with mainstream retail developments.

Skills

The change to a retailing culture demands entirely new skills in branch offices. Traditionally, branch office staff were content to offer their customers an efficient local service; staff who showed signs of ability would have been transferred to larger branches or, eventually, to head-office, while the professional specialists would have been concentrated in head-office or regional-office teams to provide a central service.

Branches now have the responsibility of marketing their products and services aggressively and training and staff development should take account of this. The Speedwing survey asked local travel agents to provide details of the number of staff, their qualifications, experience and training record to date. These figures were compared with the forecast numbers and skills needed to run an effective sales and marketing operation in different size outlets. It was possible to develop a target branch skills profile and to identify the training needs for that branch.

Management structure

Management skills also need to be developed, managers have changing priorities in the new branch retailing environment; they need to gain competence in marketing, personal service, staff development and customer service as well as the inherent accounting and administrative skills. The management structure is likely to vary from branch to branch and could influence the success of the outlet. A branch where the senior manager is also the owner will have high motivation levels to achieve success and develop a level of service that meets customer needs. If the branch is large enough to support a management team, responsibility for marketing and for developing staff can be delegated.

The Speedwing survey looked at the management structure within travel agency branches to see how training could be used to improve local performance. They assessed:

- the manager's area of responsibility;
- number of staff;
- professional qualifications;
- recent training record;
- objectives;
- customer service skills training;
- retailing skills.

Using this information, they were able to develop targeted training programmes for individual managers and also to ensure that, through training, managers developed the flexibility to take on different roles within the agency network. This improved career opportunities and helped to ensure consistent standards of service throughout the network.

Customer profile

Another important variation in corporate branch performance is customer profile. By identifying the type of customers each branch deals with, it is possible to fine-tune a training and support package to develop the right combination of skills. In the Speedwing Training survey, travel agencies were asked to identify the type of business, number of customers and frequency of purchase under a number of headings:

- business travel;
- holiday travel;
- scheduled or charter business;
- special interest travel.

The principle of categorising customers can be applied to any type of business and used to develop a support programme.

OPPORTUNITIES AND PROBLEMS IN A MULTIPLE FRANCHISE ENVIRONMENT

The local support policy will vary if the distributor operates a multiple franchise – distributing the products or services of a number of different organisations. The supplier is competing for space and attention, and must build the local outlet's commitment to the product. Successful development of a multiple franchise outlet requires a number of important actions:

- getting the right level of space and attention;
- building the loyalty of the distributor;
- gaining sales staff acceptance and understanding of the company's

products and services;
- achieving a high level of participation in marketing and business development programmes;
- getting the co-operation of the distributor to invest in business development activities;
- allocating the right level of marketing support.

Competing for attention

In a multiple franchise, the distributor is under no obligation to carry any of the supplier's products; it is a matter of choice, and the distributor is likely to favour products that match his business profile and offer the best profit opportunities. The task facing the salesforce is different:

- with franchised distributors, the supplier's salesforce is helping the distributor to achieve the highest standards of performance;
- with independent distributors, the supplier's salesforce is trying to convince them to stock the products before they can attempt to improve performance.

To encourage distributors to stock their products, suppliers must demonstrate that the product will benefit the distributor's business and show that they will provide a high level of support to boost sales. To ensure that the distributor's sales staff maintains the right level of interest in the product, sales training and sales incentives must be provided as part of the overall programme.

A pitch to a national food retailer might include a number of proposals to win distribution:

- market research showing that the product was gaining market share over products already stocked by the retailer;
- product and consumer profile showing how the product will enhance the retailer's existing product range or offer new market opportunities;
- current and proposed expenditure on consumer advertising;
- sales promotion programmes specific to the retailer, including special offers, discounts and competitions;

- display material designed to integrate with the retailer's corporate identity;
- product training for the retailer's sales staff;
- incentives and discount structure.

Building loyalty

The second stage is to ensure that independent distributors continue to support the product and maintain an effective business relationship. If the supplier wants to achieve key long-term business objectives through a multiple franchise network, the support policies must be strong enough to maintain distributor loyalty. Actions to build loyalty might include:

- structured incentive programmes to encourage high levels of repeat purchase;
- strengthening of business relationships to increase the retailer's dependence on the supplier.

Gaining sales staff acceptance

To improve sales performance in a multiple franchise environment, a supplier must ensure that distributor sales staff are aware of all the features and benefits of the product range and are committed to selling them. If they are under pressure from other suppliers to sell their products, the sales staff may not give their full commitment and attention. Important actions would include:

- generating high levels of consumer enquiries through effective product advertising and sales promotion;
- ensuring that the product is easy to sell;
- providing the right level of product information;
- offering attractive sales incentive programmes.

Participating in the supplier's business programmes

Independent distributors are under no contractual obligation to participate in the supplier's business and marketing programmes that may be crucial to successful customer relations. For example, if a manufacturer wishes to offer customers a free extended warranty or discounted service as a means of winning market share, the success of the offer depends on the co-operation of the distributor in operating the programme. In launching these programmes to distributors, suppliers may have to use structured incentives to encourage participation. If distributors do not participate suppliers may not be able to achieve their overall objectives.

Investing in business development

Suppliers use skills training and business development programmes to improve the quality of distributor service to their customers. With so many potential conflicting interests, and so many product ranges to cover, a multiple franchise distributor may not be in a position to invest or commit staff to training programmes. Training represents lost selling time, so independent distributors need stronger incentives to take on time-consuming programmes. Actions include:

- discounts on training;
- free advice and guidance on business development;
- valuable recognition and award schemes linked to programme participation.

Marketing support

Marketing support has to be carefully managed to ensure it provides the optimum benefit for the supplier. If the distributor is marketing a range of competitive products, the support material may be used to improve sales of the whole of the distributor's range and not just the supplier's products. Traffic-building promotions which attract customers to a branch may be simply building sales of other products.

Although independent multi-franchise distributors offer the same business benefits as other distributors, they need to be more carefully managed if they are to contribute to the success of a supplier's overall local marketing strategy.

SUCCESS FACTORS IN LOCAL MARKETING

Given the characteristics of distributors as small local businesses, and the requirements of suppliers to offer specific levels of service to their customers, it is possible to identify a set of success factors that can be used to evaluate the potential of new outlets and to measure the performance of an existing local network. These are the key success factors, though they are not necessarily in order of importance:

- the distributor meets customer expectations;
- there are consistent standards throughout the network;
- staff and management are highly motivated;
- the network is responsive and flexible;
- the distributors are financially stable;
- the network provides broad market coverage;
- the staff have the skills to provide a quality service;
- the distributors are well managed.

Meeting customer expectations

Chapter 9 – 'Focusing on customer care' – describes the standards that customers expect in terms of convenience, quality of service, product knowledge, delivery, price and aftercare and shows how suppliers can use customer focus standards to help distributors provide the right level of customer care. Before a supplier can improve customer care standards, it must be aware of customers' real needs and these can be identified through research and through customer satisfaction surveys.

By continually measuring customer satisfaction performance, a supplier can determine whether the branch is offering the right level of service and meeting customer's changing expectations. These customer expectations may vary at national and local level, so it is important to decide which has priority.

Motivated team

Motivation was shown to be a feature of small businesses, but that motivation must be channelled to meet the supplier's key business objectives. Independent multi-franchise distributors may be highly motivated, but if they believe the rewards are greater from other suppliers, they may not be fully committed to one particular product range. Motivation must be developed throughout the local team, because high levels of customer satisfaction depend on a quality service from every member of a team.

Responsive

The local network must be able to respond quickly to changes in business conditions. This is not simply a question of attitude, local outlets must be assessing the changing needs of their customers, continuously, and suppliers must be aware of both local and national changes so that they can make appropriate changes in pricing, product range, delivery and standards. Flexibility depends on good information flow between suppliers and local outlets and a rapid decision-making process which will enable both parties to respond rapidly to threats and opportunities.

Financially stable

A local outlet that is financially stable is able to provide a guaranteed long-term service to the supplier's local customers. It also has the resources to invest in business development to meet changing customer requirements for increasing standards of customer service. The supplier contributes to this by operating effective pricing and discount policies to enable the distributor to earn a reasonable margin, and by providing marketing and business support to improve turnover and profit and run an efficient business.

Broad market coverage

The local network must enable the supplier to reach its whole customer base cost-effectively. It must provide the right geographical coverage and also provide local customers with the product knowledge and quality of service they expect from the supplier. Marketing policies and participation agreements must be acceptable to the local outlets so that they are willing to implement the whole programme and enable the supplier to cover the entire market.

Skilled staff

Quality service depends on quality staff and this is a key factor in determining the success of a local network. Skilled staff can handle customer enquiries efficiently by demonstrating the right level of product knowledge. Good customer-handling skills and understanding of customer care contribute to high levels of customer satisfaction and the skills to carry out efficient service delivery across the after-sales cycle.

Well managed

Good skills don't just apply to the staff who deliver the service, effective management can ensure that the right resources are committed to the supplier's products and that the local outlet invests in an infrastructure that provides the highest quality of service to the customer and continues to deliver an efficient profitable service.

Consistent standards

A support programme succeeds when it enables the local network to deliver consistent standards of customer service at each outlet. This does not mean delivering the same standard service because the requirements of each market may vary, but delivering the key elements that affect customer satisfaction and loyalty.

Developing support to achieve the success factors

These factors provide valuable guidelines for developing support programmes to improve local marketing performance. Before looking at the way in which support can be used to develop independent small businesses, we will look at the way in which national support policies can be used as part of an integrated strategy.

THE CONTRIBUTION OF NATIONAL SUPPORT POLICIES

The traditional starting point for any local marketing programme is the national support programme – it treats the network as a whole and views individual outlets as elements of the whole, rather than individual businesses in their own right.

A national support policy ranks distributors in terms of their size and turnover and may allocate business and marketing support resources on the basis of comparative size. In many cases, the aim of the national support programme is to develop a homogeneous network in which every outlet appears to be the same – the kind of policy that led to such blandness and uniformity in shopping mall developments of the mid-1980s. This is not to deny the value of national support policies, because they may have important business benefits, but there are risks in adopting a policy that ignores differences in local marketing conditions. There are a number of important benefits to a national support policy:

- they ensure that customers expect a consistent service wherever they go, essential to hotels and food chains for example;
- they enable a strong branding policy so that companies can take advantage of national advertising programmes to raise awareness of a whole distributor network;
- they ensure that customers who require a service in different areas, petrol buyers for example, or car hirers, will enjoy the same standards of service;
- they help a company to grow its network by replicating standards in new locations;
- they help to build a coherent network when a company is growing by merger and acquisition;
- they enable a company to bid for multi-site contracts by allowing it to offer a consistent service on each site.

Convenience for customers

When customers are selecting a supplier, they want to feel confident that they are making the right choice. Take a travel agent or a hotel group, for example; what kind of reputation do they have, will customers be assured of the same standards of service and what should they expect? By imposing standards and developing consistent standards of service at every outlet, the head-office team can control quality and meet customer expectations throughout the network.

Branding

Consistent standards enable a company to develop a brand for its local network in the same way as it brands products. Brand values help the supplier to manage perceptions of its local network by running national advertising campaigns to attract customers to its distributor network. Brand values work only if the individual outlets are able to meet the quality of service.

Different locations

'Travelling services' such as petrol stations represent frequent purchase decisions where customers have a choice and benefit directly from a consistent national standard. A motorist wants to know that wherever he uses a particular petrol station, he will enjoy the same product and the same standard of service. Although petrol is a commodity, it is the other facilities at the petrol station that provide the added value and enable the individual petrol station to attract and retain customers.

Growing a network

When a company is in a growth phase, building its local network, it is helpful to be able to replicate the quality of service and the key success factors across a complete network.

Rationalising a network

The same comments apply when a manufacturer is rationalising a group of local outlets that have grown through acquisition and merger. Each of them may be operating different standards and the supplier needs to be certain that it can offer consistency of standards across the network.

Handling multi-site customers

In industrial distributor networks, a customer may place a contract that involves the distribution of products and services across a large number of different outlets. To ensure that the service is delivered consistently across all the outlets, stringent policies would need to be applied. National support policies can help to meet the requirements of this market.

SUMMARY

This chapter explains the reasons why local outlets are important and outlines the important benefits to companies supplying both products and services. It explains why local outlets should be treated as independent small businesses, rather than outposts of head office, and analyses the strengths and weaknesses of the approach. It then looks in more detail at specific opportunities and problems in applying the principle of independent businesses to branch offices and independent multiple franchise outlets. The chapter then considers the success factors that can be used to measure the potential of a local outlet as an independent business. Finally, it shows how traditional support policies go only part of the way to meeting the criteria for developing successful local businesses.

ACTION CHECKLIST

You may find this checklist useful in evaluating the potential of your own local network. The questions can easily be customised to your market sector and will form the basis for planning and delegation. If you need further information on any aspect of the questions, the topics broadly follow the sequence of the chapter.

YOUR SALESFORCE

How important are local outlets to your business?

Do you have a direct salesforce and how well does it cover your market?

Is the direct salesforce stretched and could some of its tasks be handled by local outlets?

Do you have the resources to handle direct sales in your international markets?

Does the national sales company in your international markets have its own salesforce?

Does your customer base divide easily into sectors that can be handled directly and through local outlets?

LOCAL INFORMATION

How well do you understand local markets?

Can you use national research companies to handle research in international markets?

Does your research enable you to identify local market patterns?

How much information do you have on competitors at local and national level?

How often do you monitor local competitive information?

DECISION MAKING

Do your corporate decision-making processes allow you to respond quickly to change?

How much responsibility do you delegate to your local outlets?

What is the decision-making process in your international markets? Do the national companies have autonomy or are they subject to central control?

CUSTOMER RELATIONSHIPS

How important are long-term customer relationships to your business?

Do you have a policy and the resources to build effective relationships?

How could your branches help you improve relationships?

PRODUCT/MARKET VARIATIONS

Do you have a standard product range or can it be modified for local markets?

What level of product variation already exists?

Is any manufacturing carried out in local markets?

LOCAL OWNERSHIP

Are your local outlets run by managers or entrepreneurs?

What is the average number of staff in a local outlet?

How much participation do local outlets have in decision making?

Are your outlets self-contained businesses or do local staff have the opportunity to transfer between different outlets?

Do different outlets within your network have the opportunity to meet to review business opportunities and problems?

What level of risk do the local businesses have and are they responsible for protecting that risk?

CONTROL

What is the relationship between you and your network and what level of control do you have?

Is your local network responsible for its own finances and how effective is its financial management?

Can you identify enough consistent factors in your network to brand it?

Could you take the strengths of your network and use them to build new outlets on a successful formula?

Is your network dependent on individuals for its current and future performance?

CORPORATE NETWORKS

Do you operate a corporate branch network and what is its scope?

Do the branches have profit responsibility?

What opportunities are there to develop business through the branches?

Are your branches retail-oriented? Do they need to be?

What changes would you have to make to create a retail environment?

Do you have the staff and management skills to develop your corporate network?

Can you use technology to improve the sales and customer service performance of your corporate network?

What are the major variations between your branches and how crucial are those factors to overall success?

MULTIPLE FRANCHISE OUTLETS

Do you deal with multiple franchise outlets and do you know what percentage of their business your sales represent?

Do they deal with your competitors and how does their share compare with yours?

What conditions do the outlets impose on you, and how does that impact on your level of business with them?

What can you do to improve the loyalty of multiple franchise outlets?

Can you increase your control over those outlets?

SUCCESS FACTORS

What are the success factors in your local outlets?

What are your customers' expectations of the service they get from your local outlets?

How can you improve those success factors?

Does your current support programme focus on those success factors?

NATIONAL SUPPORT POLICIES

Do you operate standard national support policies?

Can you operate standard programmes across an international network?

How well branded are your outlets?

Are your standards of customer satisfaction sufficiently high?

Do your customers visit a number of different outlets within the network?

Do you need to impose overall standards on the network to reduce performance scatter?

2

AGENDA FOR LOCAL MARKETING

INTRODUCTION

The first chapter explained the importance of effective local marketing. The remainder of the book provides a basis for planning and implementing programmes that help to achieve the right level of local service. The chapter also explained the key performance factors that need to be managed and this needs to be discussed at a senior level within the company to develop an effective local marketing strategy.

This chapter is structured as an agenda for reviewing the current situation, setting objectives and evaluating support options. The remaining chapters look at the options in more detail. The agenda covers the following topics:

- importance of local markets to your organisation;
- scope of network plans;
- current status of your network;
- reasons for action;
- current performance and targets;
- operating constraints;
- competitive activity;
- current support programmes; additional support requirements;
- resources;
- support priorities;
- timetable for change;
- planned perceptions.

IMPORTANCE OF LOCAL MARKETS

Chapter 1 described how effective local marketing could help a supplier to improve overall marketing performance. It described key benefits including:

- supplementing a direct salesforce;
- better understanding of local markets and changing customer requirements;
- greater awareness of local competitors and individual actions to deal with competitive threats;
- rapid and effective response to change in the marketplace or to specific customer requirements;
- opportunity to build close personal working relationships with individual customers, essential in building and retaining long-term business;
- better local knowledge to tailor products or services to the local market;
- small effective teams that can operate flexibly in the changing conditions of the local market.

The first stage in setting your local marketing objectives is to decide which of these factors are most important to your overall corporate objectives.

- Would you be able to improve sales by recruiting additional direct-sales staff, for example, and training them to sell what may be a complex product? The investment in expanding and supporting a local network with an ongoing programme of training may not provide the results you want.
- Are your long-term business objectives focused on the same markets that your local outlets offer you, or are you moving in a completely different direction? For example, a manufacturing company that has taken a strategic decision to become a services company to support its customer base is likely to need an entirely different type of local network from the one that may already be established.
- If your customers are moving to Just-in-Time manufacturing, will this influence the shape of the network you need? Would it be

better to invest in improved communications and logistics in partnership with customers?

- If you are in consumer retailing, is home shopping likely to
influence your future business prospects? Can you afford to invest
in bricks and mortar when you should be considering sophisticated
electronic payments systems?

This is not to decry the importance of local outlets, but to ensure that
executives consider them within the context of future developments
in the marketplace and in marketing technology so that their investment is not wasted.

Midland Bank's First Direct telephone banking service has
captured valuable market share since its launch, but it is unlikely to
spell the end of local branch banking as we know it. What it has shown
is that there are different ways to deliver a banking service and that
there is a strong consumer demand for a highly personal, highly
flexible service that is completely different to traditional counter
services.

SCOPE OF YOUR NETWORK PLANS

Local outlets remain a vital element in the marketing mix, but you
need to define what you mean by a local service. Your plans will be
determined by the geographical scope of your network and the
resources needed to support it.

- Does it serve all your customers in one specific region or are you
attempting to provide national or international coverage? A
regional building society may have national ambitions but the
resources to achieve that are considerably greater.
- Do you have the skills to set up and manage a large network or
should you concentrate on growing the business within your established market?
- Have your existing outlets reached their full potential or would you
be better to concentrate on introducing new products and services
or improving the outlets' performance?
- Do you have the opportunity to develop strategic alliances with

other groups that run networks in other regions or countries? This may be a better alternative to growing your own network.

- Are there pressing reasons for going outside your current region – better marketing opportunities, faster growth, weaker competition?
- You may, on the other hand, be rationalising your network and coming out of a major distribution operation to concentrate on key territories and core activities. Running a global network may be an unnecessary strain on resources which does not provide a justifiable return.

Saatchi and Saatchi grew from a highly-respected UK advertising agency to the largest advertising group in the world, offering their clients an agency service in every one of the world's main markets. This global presence was a logical stage in the development of the advertising industry as clients put an increasing emphasis on global brands and demanded agencies that could produce consistently high standards of advertising in every important consumer market. Like many of the global advertising groups, Saatchi and Saatchi grew by acquiring national and international agency groups, with each deal growing progressively larger. However, advertising is a highly personal business run by strong-minded individuals and the problems of trying to control a disparate group of individualistic companies across such far-reaching boundaries contributed to the crisis the group faced at the end of the '80s. The strategy of growing rapidly to compete as a global player was right but the problems of trying to maintain tight control proved too much.

CURRENT STATUS OF YOUR NETWORK

Before developing plans for growth or rationalisation, it is essential to analyse the current status of your local network. If you don't you run the risk of focusing on the wrong problems.

- You may not yet have a network, but you have identified important opportunities a network will provide and you are beginning with a clean sheet. Chapter 3 provides useful information on presenting your requirements and opportunities to potential distributors. Your tasks will be greater than companies who are seeking to improve the performance of their network because you will have to determine the type of network you need, assess potential candidates and then establish the level of performance you want.

- If your network is incomplete, you need to identify the factors that have been successful so far and see where you can replicate them in a cost-effective way to achieve the coverage you need.
- The network may be complete, but performing inconsistently or poorly; your discussions should focus on the priorities for business development and the next chapter deals with this in more detail.
- If you are rationalising your network, you need to have a clear view of the level of service your customers require so that you can rationalise without sacrificing quality. Chapter 9 gives clear guidelines on the way to assess customer standards and ensure that local outlets continue to deliver the right level of service.

The Arlington Motor Company was a disparate group of dealerships with inconsistent levels of performance and an over-dependence on the quality of local dealer principals. The company's long-term strategy was to increase the number of outlets through acquisition so that it could offer a powerful regional service to large fleet operators. However, the group realised that it had to overcome the problem of 'performance scatter' in its existing outlets before it embarked on expansion plans. This decision helped to focus the group on its immediate problems before it tackled the more difficult task of trying to integrate new dealerships into a network.

REASONS FOR ACTION

Whatever the status of the network, have you identified why it needs to be improved? Many companies make the mistake of increasing the local advertising budgets as a gesture to distributor support when the money could have been better spent on, say, appointing a distributor specialist to maintain high levels of contact with local outlets and work with them to improve their own business. Local outlets might need greater incentives or more training to meet their performance requirements. By analysing current performance and identifying the key areas for improvement, you will be able to develop the correct strategy.

These scenarios outline some improvement programmes you might tackle.

- You have an established network which meets quality and customer service standards, but you want to improve the level of sales. The emphasis will be on sales incentives or promotional support to generate enquiries.
- You want to broaden the range of products or services available through your branch. As well as selling those products into the branch, you will have to operate training programmes to ensure local staff understand the products and the market opportunities.
- You are trying to improve the quality of service or the consistency of service available from the network. Your efforts will be focused on providing training and programmes to improve performance and you will need to monitor standards through effective local management and customer satisfaction surveys.
- You are trying to improve your coverage of the market. You can achieve this by increasing the number of branches, if that is a practical proposition, or by working in partnership with your local outlets to develop their business and improve market performance.

When Case Europe, the construction and agricultural equipment manufacturer, wanted to ensure the reliability of its equipment in the field, it identified a need to ensure that customers bought only genuine quality replacement parts. Customers had been fitting cheaper substitute parts and suffering increased downtime through breakdowns. To ensure that customers could get the parts they needed, Case had to take action at a number of different levels:

- stress the importance, through advertising, of buying genuine quality parts from an authorised distributor;
- ensure that their distributors stocked a comprehensive range of parts;
- improve levels of professionalism and customer service throughout

their distributor network so that their distributors were perceived as first choice for parts and service.

They could have relied on an advertising campaign to get across the message about the importance of quality products, but they knew that distributor performance would be critical to building a reputation for professionalism.

MANAGING PERFORMANCE

The scenarios in the last section provide a basis for setting local marketing support objectives, but they must be converted into quantifiable targets which can be measured and managed effectively. Taking sales as an example:

- Do you want to raise overall volume or increase sales of strategic products or services that ensure customer loyalty?
- Do you want to raise sales across the network or bring under-performing outlets up to the standard of the rest of the network?

Chapter 5, 'Developing a local marketing plan', explains the importance of sector marketing. That means working closely with local outlets to help them identify their key tasks and ensuring that they adhere to those standards. For example, if your aim is to improve the quality of customer service, this can be expressed as a vague intention to do better, or as a series of achievable and measurable targets such as:

- improve levels of customer service at every branch;
- increase opening hours;
- operate x per cent more customer programmes.

Arlington Motors' approach to the problem of 'performance scatter' described earlier in this chapter was to introduce consistent benchmark standards to every dealership so that comparative performance could be measured and understood by everyone in the network. Before the introduction of those standards, no one in the head-office team had understood why there was such a difference in performance between individual outlets.

OPERATING CONSTRAINTS

The degree of control you can exercise over your local network depends on whether it is independent or franchised. Franchised distributors, wholly-owned subsidiaries or branches have to partici- pate in your key business development programmes. Because of the nature of their relationship, you have direct control over them. But if the outlets are independent you will have to commit more resources to persuade them to participate in programmes and build their loyalty to your company. Independent distributors may give you solus distribution on your products or they may carry a range of competitive products and play one supplier off against another. You need to decide how important distributor control is to achieving your overall objectives and develop a strategy for achieving that control.

- You may decide to take a financial stake in the distributor network so that you have a controlling interest or you may simply increase the level of representation to ensure you can influence decisions.
- An increasing number of manufacturers are linking levels of distributor or branch support to the achievement of effective cus- tomer satisfaction levels that meet national business objectives.

COMPETITIVE ACTIVITY

Comparing the performance of your distributor network against your competitors' not only gives you a benchmark for performance, but also highlights threats or opportunities you might not have been aware of.

- Do your competitors have a local network? If not, what do they do instead?
- What do their customers think of their local network?
- Is your network inferior in some way and is that seen by customers and prospects as a barrier to doing business with you?
- Do competitors offer a national or international network which makes them more credible or more acceptable to large corporate clients?

- How do they structure their network – is it through a loose association or does it have a corporate structure of its own which can be tightly controlled?

You need to be aware of your competitors' strengths and weaknesses in your own local markets.

- Do they have a presence there and does it threaten your outlets' business?
- Are they introducing national development programmes which will work their way through to your local market and threaten your business?

Chapter 4, 'Assessing local market opportunities', provides more detail on how to assess the level of competition.

CURRENT SUPPORT

The analysis of network performance and competitive activity will highlight areas where you need to make improvements or provide higher levels of support. Before planning a programme for future support, you need to assess current levels of support and decide how well it is helping your local outlets to meet their objectives.

- Does your current advertising programme raise the profile of your local network and does it generate the right level of enquiries to build local sales?
- Have you got training programmes in position to help distributors reach the skills levels you have set, and are the incentive programmes actually helping local outlets achieve their sales targets?
- Does your current support programme operate evenly across the network, or is your programme focused on selected outlets, leading to an imbalance in performance?
- Do your support programmes represent value for money or could they be managed more effectively? For example, if you provide funds direct to local outlets to run their own advertisements, would it be better to operate a central local advertising operation and use the accumulated funds to get better discounts from the media?

- Is the impact of your total spend being weakened because local outlets put out individual messages and there is no benefit from cumulative and consistent marketing activities integrated across the whole network?

One of the biggest changes in car marketing occurred when Kevin Morley, a director of the Rover Group, left the company to set up an advertising agency to handle all of the Rover Group's advertising and marketing activities. This included national consumer advertising, dealer support, sales promotion, parts and service support and a host of other activities. All of these activities had been handled by separate suppliers in the past, giving Rover a major co-ordination task and potentially weakening the strength of its corporate image. The new agency's solution was to provide a single integrated marketing solution across the whole promotional spectrum. This enabled Rover to provide a consistent quality of support to its dealer network and strengthen its position in the market by making the most effective use of its support resources.

ADDITIONAL SUPPORT REQUIREMENTS

Chapters 4 and 6, 'Assessing market opportunities' and 'Assessing support requirements', will ensure that your support activities are aligned to your network's business and marketing objectives. Chapter 5, 'Developing a local marketing plan', will help to identify the essential support activities at a local level and these can be integrated into a national plan.

- If a large number of outlets need to develop higher skill levels, you may decide to set up a training centre of your own or work in conjunction with a group of training specialists to develop a customised training service for your outlets.
- If you are expanding your operations to build a national or international network, the nature of the support programme will change considerably and you will need to focus on long-term branding of the network and establishing new outlets rather than aiming at short-term tactical sales increases.

- Have you monitored competitors' support activities to see how they support their outlets? They may be able to provide an insight into techniques that enable you to improve your own support programmes.

RESOURCES

How you tailor your support programmes depends on the resources you have available and how much you are prepared to commit to the performance of your local markets.

- Are local sales handled by the general salesforce or do you have a specialist who is responsible for local branch development? Chapter 11, 'Developing a contact strategy', explains the role that a distributor specialist might have and shows how much emphasis local branches put on the value of regular contact.
- As well as staff to maintain contact with local outlets, you also need to have people with the professional skills to manage or deliver the support programmes. If you intend to operate all the support programmes in-house, you will be committed to staff costs and equipment as Chapter 14, 'Controlling local support programmes', shows, but the costs can be controlled by outsourcing an agency service to deliver essential services.
- You will have to allocate budgets for marketing activities and set aside funds for investment and improvement of facilities where the return on investment can be justified.

If you do not have sufficient resources to handle your local marketing development programme properly it may fail, so it is important to assess these correctly. The example of the Rover Group agency which handled all marketing support activities demonstrates the increasing importance that companies put on their local support activities. In the past, these have been relegated to lowly status and starved of essential budgets. Few advertising agencies have shown an interest in local support advertising so the area has been neglected.

SUPPORT PRIORITIES

If you are operating a large network you may have to deal with conflicting demands or you may not have the resources to handle all the demands on you. It is important to establish priorities and to align these with key business and marketing objectives.

- If your overall aim is to achieve the highest levels of customer satisfaction, then you would allocate resources to programmes that help to improve customer satisfaction and loyalty.
  - the budget in year one might be allocated to setting customer standards and launching them to distributors;
  - part of the budget after the launch would be taken up by customer-care training and support programmes that enable local branches to communicate customer care in the marketplace;
  - in later years, the budget would be allocated to recognised incentive programmes that enabled manufacturers to encourage higher levels of performance.
- Customer loyalty programmes would have the highest importance if distributors are suffering from low levels of repeat business and a high turnover of customers.
- If the company is introducing new products or expanding its customer base, new business development programmes have the highest priority.

Support levels and priorities are fine-tuned to the needs of the local market and to the key sales development tasks.

TIMETABLE

As well as allocating priorities, you also need to determine your short and long-term objectives and to establish a timetable for achieving key distributor objectives.

- If, for example, you aim to establish your network as the market leader in a number of market sectors, this is not likely to be a short-term programme. In your assessment of the market, you will be laying down the long-term skills and service levels needed to succeed and investing in the training and service infrastructure that will ensure success.

- Shorter-term tactical promotions and sales campaigns will help to boost turnover and profit, but they could divert resources away from the strategic tasks.
- Advertising and direct mail programmes have their own production lead times built in and they must be planned to coincide with the peak buying times.

PLANNED PERCEPTIONS

As Chapter 5, 'Developing a local marketing plan', shows, it is important to have a specific perception of the network in mind to guide the support activities. This will not only help to establish the support priorities and the levels of support needed, it will also determine how the standards are to be achieved and will provide a target for local outlets. Like all other objectives, it must be translated into tangible benefits and actions so that it works. These are some examples of that target perception and the supporting actions:

- our network offers the highest standards of service anywhere in the country;
- you will get the same quality of service wherever you go;
- we offer the best selection of products in Europe;
- now you can enjoy the same standards of service throughout Europe;
- we aim to set the best local delivery standards of service in the business;
- you will have a personal guarantee of satisfaction backed by an unconditional exchange scheme anywhere.

These are promises that cannot be achieved without a great deal of hard work and support, but they enable the manufacturer and the distributor to work together to achieve those standards.

SUMMARY

This chapter has provided an outline of the important issues you need to discuss before you plan and implement a local marketing support programme. It explains that you need to integrate your local support objectives with your overall business objectives and identify the priorities. The chapter emphasises the importance of issues such as customer satisfaction and shows how priorities will vary depending on the current status of your network. This chapter is structured as an agenda to help you review the current status of your local network and set objectives for improving performance. The first part helps you evaluate the importance of local markets to your organisation and asks you to consider whether your local network will continue to meet your changing needs. The section, 'Scope of your network plans' looks at the geographical context of networks and asks you to consider whether you have the resources to support your plans. By analysing the current status of your network, you can focus on the right priorities, rather than heading in the wrong direction. The section, 'Reasons for action' provides a number of scenarios to help you identify your most important development tasks. The next section recommends turning those tasks into quantifiable activities by measuring current performance and setting specific targets. The section on operating constraints asks you to consider whether you need to strengthen the degree of control over your local outlets before implementing improvement plans. You must also assess the likely impact of competitive activity on your plans. By assessing your current support programmes, you will be able to identify additional support requirements and quantify the resources you need to provide support. The chapter recommends that you establish support priorities and establish a timetable for change. Finally, the chapter asks you to state the planned perception for your local network – how you want customers to view it.

ACTION CHECKLIST

This chapter is already in the form of an agenda, but for convenience we have extracted some of the more important questions for inclusion in the checklist.

IMPORTANCE OF LOCAL OUTLETS

Does your local market profile fit your long-term strategy?

What trends might affect the long-term shape of your network?

Are there viable alternatives to your current network?

Are any of your competitors utilising other forms of local marketing?

SCOPE OF THE NETWORK

Are your plans regional, national or international?

Do you aim to grow organically or would acquisition be more appropriate?

Are there any significant barriers to growth?

Are there alternative strategies to growing the local network?

Do you have the resources to manage growth?

CURRENT STATUS

Is your network new, incomplete or complete?

Are you a new entrant to the market in new territories?

What plans do you have to change the status of the network?

Is the performance of the network satisfactory?

Are your international outlets established or are you starting from scratch?

Can you measure the performance of your network with confidence?

REASONS FOR ACTION

What are the main reasons for making changes to your network?

What benefits do you see from those changes?

How essential or urgent are the changes?

Are the planned changes dealing with the right issues?

Do the reasons for action vary across your international network?

MANAGING PERFORMANCE

Can you measure performance of key factors across your network?

What can you do to improve your capability to measure performance?

Have you got benchmarks for your key performance standards?

Are your targets measurable and do they form a valid basis for comparison of different outlets?

Do your performance measurements vary across international markets?

Do your performance standards allow for start-ups in new territories?

OPERATING CONSTRAINTS

Can you improve control over outlets where you have no direct influence?

Do international management structures impose constraints?

Are you constrained by national business conditions or legislation in international markets?

Can you link support levels to achievements of any other performance criteria such as customer satisfaction levels?

Are there any other constraints that impact on your plans?

COMPETITIVE ACTIVITY

Does competitive activity threaten the current or future success of your network?

How does your competitors' local marketing performance compare with yours?

What are their key success factors?

Can you adopt any of your competitors' practices to benefit your own network?

What actions are you taking against competitors, and how successful are they?

Do you face strong domestic competition in international markets?

CURRENT SUPPORT

How effective is your support programme?

Are you changing it because your business objectives are changing?

What factors influence the success of your current support programme?

Can your current support programmes be utilised in international markets?

Are support budgets or resources a barrier to improving performance?

ADDITIONAL SUPPORT REQUIREMENTS

What additional forms of support would you introduce if you had a free choice?

What other forms of support can you introduce within your budget and resource limitations?

Do your international markets require additional forms of support?

What are the support priorities in different markets?

Are any competitive support programmes appropriate to your network?

RESOURCES

Do you have the resources to handle local marketing effectively?

Have you analysed your in-house support costs and compared them with the costs of an external agency?

Do you have local skills and resources to handle international marketing tasks?

Are there any support activities that could be handled cost effectively by external sources?

SUPPORT PRIORITIES

How well do current support activities reflect your overall objectives?

How important are your support objectives?

How can you prioritise the tasks?

Do priorities vary in international markets?

TIMETABLE FOR CHANGE

How urgent are the activities in your programme?

What is your timescale for achieving change?

Which are the most critical items in the programme?

Is your timetable affected by production lead times?

PLANNED PERCEPTIONS

What are your planned perceptions for your network?

Will these perceptions vary by territory in your international markets?

How do they reflect your customers' expectations?

How well is your support programme aligned to your target perceptions?

3

FOCUSING ON THE NEEDS OF LOCAL OUTLETS

INTRODUCTION

Marketing through local outlets is not a one-way process; it should be mutually beneficial, where suppliers achieve the standard of performance they need to meet their customers' requirements and the local outlets get the support and the backing to build their own successful business.

This chapter outlines what local outlets are looking for in a relationship and shows how suppliers can present that information to the local outlet's management team. The key elements include:

- products give broad market coverage;
- products move quickly;
- comprehensive product information is available;
- the company has a clear marketing direction;
- the local outlet will be updated on company developments;
- the supplier will maintain regular contact at all levels;
- high levels of technical support are available;
- training is comprehensive and convenient;
- local outlets can provide input into marketing support programmes;
- the supplier will help to build distributor traffic;
- the supplier runs customer loyalty programmes;
- sales incentive schemes are available;
- recognition programmes help to build commitment within the local outlet;
- business and marketing programmes are simple to administer.

The importance of these factors will vary with the type of local network you are developing and the current status of your network, but they can be modified and incorporated into a comprehensive support programme.

PRODUCTS GIVE BROAD MARKET COVERAGE

Local outlets want to know that the product range they are distributing will provide full coverage of the local market. If the supplier can meet all the local outlet's product requirements, that will simplify administration, ordering and business development by providing a single source solution. If the supplier complements products from other manufacturers they should make a good fit with the rest of the range. The broader the product range, the larger the market opportunities for the distributor and this should be communicated clearly.

Whole market coverage

A components manufacturer, for example, might stress that the products in the range provide coverage of a high percentage of applications. Manufacturers of spark plugs or car wiper blades frequently claim that their products cover 75 per cent of the European market. This means that the local outlet's potential market is very large and this is a major advantage provided it does not require large stock holding.

Rationalised range/high coverage

A far better offer is to cover 75 per cent of the European market with a rationalised range of just 12 products. The local outlet is able to attract the same potential market, but with a lower stock cost and simple product retrieval.

New market opportunities

Local outlets are also looking for products that take them into different segments of the market. An electrical distributor that has traditionally dealt with low-cost, fast-moving consumer goods may look for high-value products that enable it to broaden its own customer profile.

Matching customer profiles

Alternatively, the local outlet may have a very precise customer profile and needs to be certain that the manufacturer's range provides the best possible fit for that market. Product and market information will help to build that understanding.

Impact on the outlet

The importance of the product range and market coverage will vary with the status of the local outlet.

- A franchised outlet selling exclusive single brands needs to know from the outset that it is not being locked into an arrangement that will limit the potential for growth.
- An independent outlet handling multiple products can integrate a new range with existing products and develop a marketing strategy from a number of different sources.

FAST-MOVING PRODUCTS

Local outlets want to know that the products they stock are easy to sell and will not sit on the shelf costing money. Products that are well branded and well supported will therefore have higher appeal than products that are unknown.

Consumer products

Before supermarkets stock a new product line, they need to be convinced that it is worth allocating valuable shelf space to the product. The supplier has to put together a presentation showing how the product will be supported with local and national advertising, explaining how successful the product is in terms of market share, describing the level of in-store support, packaging and other promotional activity to attract customers. Sales promotion and product support are described in more detail later in this chapter and they are an essential element in gaining the commitment of a retail outlet.

Industrial distribution

In industrial distribution, the trend is to rationalise the number of product lines while maintaining stock cover so that distributors can improve their turnover and profitability. A supplier's proposal should demonstrate how the complete package of product and marketing support will help to boost business by attracting higher levels of business and faster turnover.

Case Europe introduced a number of measures into its European distributor support programme to improve turnover:

- it redesigned many of the outlets to incorporate self-service facilities and launched a new range of fast-moving products such as workwear, oil and accessories suitable for a retail environment;
- it helped distributors to negotiate contracts with local service outlets to supply volume parts for scheduled servicing and repairs;
- it developed structured long-term incentive programmes to encourage higher levels of repeat purchase.

Service marketing

While product performance can be monitored and translated into a local support plan, services are more difficult to quantify in terms of their turnover. Delivering services efficiently takes considerable training and investment in service infrastructure, so local outlets need to know the investment will be justified in terms of higher levels of business.

Service business can be regular in the case of scheduled servicing or ad hoc in terms of repair and maintenance. Local outlets need clear guidelines on the volume of service they will be handling and they need to know that the supplier is actively promoting the value of scheduled servicing and quality repairs through a recognised outlet. Service is something that is easily overlooked and it requires high levels of generic promotion and special service offers to attract customers.

Companies such as Halfords have made a major impact on the car servicing market by branding their service and making service easier to buy. Consumers who were afraid of large bills from service outlets had perhaps postponed service or neglected it. Now they were reassured by clearly priced service options. Instead of making customers pay a single large sum for an all-inclusive major service, Halfords offered a choice of service modules – an oil change, tune-up, safety check, intermediate service – all fully itemised and all carrying a fixed price. It made it easier for customers to buy service at affordable prices and increased the level of service business.

COMPREHENSIVE PRODUCT INFORMATION

Local outlets need to understand the products they are handling so that they can deliver a high standard of service to their customers and so that they can fully exploit the marketing opportunities that the product offers. Product information is also important to help local outlets communicate with their customers. When customers complain that 'the salesforce didn't understand what they were trying to sell me', it is a sure sign that the supplier has failed to communicate the right level of product knowledge.

Easy-to-use salesforce information

Local outlets want information in a form that is easy to access and easy to use. A company that sends out comprehensive product guides in the form of a voluminous ring binder may be fulfilling an obligation to provide product information, but if the information is unmanageable, the binder may be left unused and the whole exercise wasted. On the other hand, a pocket reference guide that gives key product features and benefits at a glance can provide a member of the local salesforce with vital information that may clinch a sale.

It is reasonable to assume that a high proportion of distributor sales staff may be casual, particularly in organisations selling consumer products with the highest levels of business at the weekend, or if the staff work on a part-time basis. In those circumstances, local outlets may find it hard to commit resources to serious training or to motivate staff to participate in training. Product information must therefore be easy to use.

Product information at the point-of-sale

An alternative to product training and salesforce product guides is to provide the right level of information to customers in the form of displays, product literature or other forms of communication which will help them to understand the benefits of the product. New technology is increasingly used to present product information in a way that involves both customer and sales staff. Interactive video, for example, enables customers and staff to work through a series of structured questions and answers that lead them to the ideal product choice.

Effective product information is a vital ingredient in building the right relationship with the customer.

CLEAR CORPORATE DIRECTION

Many local outlets complain that they are not aware of the direction their suppliers are taking. What products do they plan to introduce and what standards will they expect in the future? Without clear guidelines, the local outlets argue they cannot plan the future of their own business and they cannot invest in an infrastructure that will support future growth. Local outlets are therefore looking for a clear sense of direction so that they can introduce a degree of certainty into the planning process. Although plans may change in detail, it is important that local outlets get an overall indication of a supplier's direction.

Achieving market leadership

'We intend to become one of the world's leading sportswear brands; we are already number one in the UK and our international development programme will ensure planned success in key international markets and will help to develop a global brand.'

To achieve world leadership and successful global branding means that the supplier will be investing considerable sums of money on supporting its products and raising consumer awareness. This will help to attract customers to the brand and should build the business in the future. The company is demonstrating its commitment to the future success of its products and that can encourage local outlets to develop their own business.

Introducing new products

We intend to introduce a new range of fast-moving industrial components that will reach the high-volume markets. To take advantage of the business opportunities, our local outlets will need to introduce new self-service merchandising techniques and to run priced customer advertisements.'

This gives local outlets a clear indication of the supplier's plans for marketing products. Instead of concentrating on specialist low-volume individual products, the supplier intends to compete in high-volume sectors and that means a change of sales technique in the local outlet. The local management team can plan its own training and sales development programme to meet the new requirements.

Introducing new technology

'From next year we will be introducing a new range of electronically-controlled machine tools. These will ensure improved reliability, but the service requirements will become more complex. To ensure that customers receive the right standards of service, we will be setting up specialist training courses for local staff in new servicing techniques.'

This tells local outlets that they will have to acquire new skills to handle future business and gives them the opportunity to plan their short-term training requirements.

Organisational change

'The company has recently merged with a major international group which will provide substantial financial backing plus the worldwide research facilities to enable it to develop a new product range.'

This statement indicates that a supplier that might have appeared risky has now acquired financial strength and other backing from its association with a large group. The local outlet can feel confident that it will continue to deal with this supplier despite recent uncertainties.

This indication of future direction helps to build distributor confidence and can improve working relationships between the two parties.

INFORMATION ON COMPANY DEVELOPMENTS

Closely related to this is keeping local outlets up to date with development within the company. Local outlets need to know about the supplier's organisation and products so that they can provide an informed service to their customers. Local outlets that deal with large organisations located in a number of different sites comment that they have difficulty in knowing who they are dealing with and who the key contacts are within different divisions.

Others claim that they are not fully aware of the range of products and services available from a supplier and they may be missing valuable marketing opportunities. A regular information service would ensure that local outlets were fully briefed on all aspects of the supplier's performance so that they could provide an informed service. Local outlets need to have information on the following areas:

- the company organisation: is it market-led and is it concentrated on the important market sectors?

- the company staff: have they got the right skills and is the company appointing the right people to fill key roles?
- any training developments within the company so that local outlets see the company is developing its own skills;
- financial performance: send copies of the latest results and update local outlets regularly on new investments or other significant financial developments. This helps to build confidence that the supplier will be able to continue providing a service;
- new product developments to keep local outlets completely up to date with the range and with any new products;
- technical bulletins to keep local outlets up to date with product performance and with any technical aspect that needs to be covered;
- organisational information so that local staff know who to contact for information on different aspects of the product, service, warranty, marketing support or other relevant information;
- new manufacturing or production developments so that local outlets know they will have continuity of supply;
- acquisitions or merger developments that might influence the future development or success of the supplier;
- advertising and marketing programmes that might impact on local business.

This information can be communicated in a number of ways:

- through the supplier's salesforce making regular visits to brief the local management team and other key personnel;
- through regular bulletins sent to key local staff;
- through regular or ad-hoc briefings.

By keeping local outlets completely up to date, suppliers can improve their working relationship and ensure that they operate in the best possible way. Hi-Tec Sports is a public company and is legally required to produce an annual report to shareholders. However, the company also takes the opportunity to send distributors a copy of the report, and its contents reflect the changes in organisation, product range, distribution, marketing and business administration that is making the company a world force. These changes have an impact on the distributor business and help to build confidence. Hi-Tec also issues an annual review of its marketing plans for the coming year. This includes information on the level of national advertising expenditure and the type of advertisements it will run, the display and promotional material available and its plans for building sales of specific product lines. Sports retailers can build their own local marketing plans around this information and take advantage of any promotional material available.

REGULAR CONTACT

Surveys have shown that local outlets welcome regular contact with suppliers at all levels. Regular contact is an essential element in keeping local staff up to date with the corporate developments described in the last two sections, but it is also an integral part of day-to-day working relationships.

International contact

In international markets, local outlets welcome the opportunity to have regular contact rather than fire-fighting visits so that they can discuss business and marketing conditions, clarify any difficult issues and keep up to date with developments. Chapter 11, 'Developing a contact strategy', shows how companies have used the resident manager to overcome the problems of distance in international distributor support.

Day-to-day queries

In the domestic market, regular contact is essential for the supplier to ensure that local outlets are aware of the full product range and are buying its products. However, local staff also appreciate the opportunity to raise queries with visiting representatives. Visits from supplier's representatives with a good technical understanding are particularly welcome because this gives both supervisors and staff the opportunity to raise queries and to provide feedback on how the supplier's products are being used.

Advice and guidance

Local staff also appreciate advice and practical support on the best way to handle new business opportunities and deal with changing market conditions. For a company that aims to provide a local marketing service this information is invaluable. It ensures that the local outlet is fully aware of its own local market and is actively developing new opportunities.

Telephone contact

Many suppliers use the telephone to supplement the efforts of their direct salesforce. A company with a small salesforce may only be able to visit monthly or even quarterly, and this may not be sufficient to achieve the right level of contact. Telephone contact on a weekly or even daily basis can help to build confidence that the supplier is fully supportive of the local outlet, and can help to build the right working relationship. The telephone contact can use a number of different strategies for maintaining regular contact – advising of deliveries, information on new products, special offers, or asking about any additional requirements before the next sales call. Local outlets that know that a supplier makes this kind of informal call are likely to build it into their ordering and administrative pattern and will use it to run their own business more efficiently.

Contact with the supplier's management team

Local staff appreciate the opportunity to make contact with the head-office management team. Most of their day-to-day contact is with the sales representative or the telephone correspondent, and those people may not have the knowledge or the authority to deal with policy queries or more serious problems in the supplier/ distributor relationship. A regional business meeting or a special event like a product launch or national sales conference provides the opportunity to make contact with the management team and this can benefit both parties. The supplier management team gets the opportunity to understand the local business at first hand and to get direct feedback on its marketing policies, while local staff can get the contact they need.

TECHNICAL SUPPORT

Local outlets see technical support as a key feature of any relationship with a supplier. Local outlets do not have substantial technical resources of their own and they depend on the manufacturer for advice and guidance and resolution of queries. Support can be at a number of levels:

- providing a high level of technical information to local outlets in the form of product guides, technical bulletins and other technical reference material. Increasingly, the information is available on computer so that it is easily accessible and can be upgraded remotely by the supplier;
- offering a technical hotline to handle immediate queries that can be resolved by telephone;
- providing a visiting technical service to deal with more complex queries;
- offering ongoing technical training courses to ensure that local staff have the right level of technical knowledge to deal with complex issues.

While these are all formal methods of providing technical support, local outlets also believe it is important to set up informal methods of technical support so that they can keep staff up to date and deal with simple queries on the spot. Technical support is one of the most important types of local support since it directly affects customer satisfaction and impacts on the perception of the distributor.

Ford Motor Company keeps its dealer service technicians up to date with new technical developments through a regular magazine that includes articles on the service implications of car technology and step-by-step guides to servicing techniques. Each edition of the magazine incorporates a quiz that enables readers to qualify for regional service skills competitions, leading to national finals. The magazine is a friendly, informal medium for getting technical information across, but it also includes useful training material and it encourages local staff to improve their skills and technical knowledge by offering a national recognition programme.

TRAINING AND DEVELOPMENT

Local staff training and development is closely related to technical support. Local outlets understand that staff are their most important asset and that effective staff can make a significant contribution to the business. However, they feel that the casual nature of the staff makes it difficult for them to be motivated by the need for training.

Accessible training

Training must be closely related to the day-to-day jobs and must be easily accessible. Courses that demand a considerable sacrifice of time and effort with no real direct reward would be seen as an imposition and residential training courses which take staff away from their duties, can impose a severe drain on local resources.

Relevant training

Local outlets prefer staff to undertake training courses that are convenient and brief – training on site or distance learning which can be carried out in their own time. Training must also be related to the job and should contribute to achieving the highest levels of customer satisfaction. Local managers believe that training and development are important, but the training must be tailored to their needs and it must help them achieve their marketing objectives.

The Speedwing Training survey, described in Chapter 1, was developed to improve the relevance of training to travel agency branches. Before the survey, the agencies had received complete information on all Speedwing Training courses and had used only part of the material. To help them manage their own training operations more effectively, Speedwing worked with them to develop a branch skills profile based on numbers of staff, current skills, training records and branch business objectives. Speedwing then sent details of only those training programmes that matched the branch's training needs and this helped to demonstrate the relevance and importance of training.

EFFECTIVE NATIONAL MARKETING SUPPORT

Local outlets want to know that suppliers support their whole business and will make strong efforts to build the business. How, for example, does a supplier plan to promote the local network – will it be through national advertising or will it be by individual outlet? If the supplier puts the largest part of the budget through product promotion rather than local marketing support, the local network may not receive the full benefit from the marketing programme.

Branding local outlets

National advertisements can help to brand local outlets so that customers are aware of the standards of service to expect from each branch. Local outlets also want to know that suppliers will be encouraging customers to use particular branches. The national advertisements would stress the generic benefits of using the group's local outlets:

- convenient locations and opening times;
- wide range of quality products and services;
- efficient personal service;
- rapid delivery from stock;
- technical excellence or reputation for quality and nationwide coverage.

These advertisements will tell customers what to expect from any outlet within the branch network; the local outlet can concentrate on carrying out its own local advertising activities with price based offers. Generic national advertising enables local outlets to take advantage of central group advertising resources which would not be available to them on an individual basis and allows them to grow the overall business through the network.

Integrating local and national support

Ideally the product, national and distributor advertisements should be totally integrated. Rover Group advertising in mid-1993 stresses the message 'above all we're Rover dealers', which is linked to the consumer car advertising message 'above all it's a Rover'. The fact that consumers see the message repeated in different formats helps to establish a strong identity for the Rover dealer network and encourages consumers to think favourably of the dealers when they are considering their next car.

Jewson, the builders merchants, ran a campaign on national television that explained the benefits of buying from any Jewson branch. It stressed the wide choice and good service, and was backed by a high-quality catalogue that stressed the same features. Local Jewson branches could run their own price or promotional advertisements and benefit from the national campaign.

LOCAL INPUT TO MARKETING PROGRAMMES

Local outlets don't like to have marketing programmes imposed on them; they prefer to have an input into the programme so that it reflects their real requirements. For example, an advertising campaign providing a new range of products may be devised by the company's advertising agency, but may not reflect the sales benefits that local staff feel are important.

The major input from local outlets would be on branch service rather than product information because they are experiencing customer reactions at first hand. By getting involved in the marketing planning process, local outlets are more likely to be committed to a particular programme because they have participated in its development and the programme is likely to succeed because it reflects the needs of the marketplace.

The information from local outlets can be gathered in a number of ways:

- through the local marketing plan, discussed in more detail in Chapter 5;
- through consultation between the distributor specialist and the local management team;
- through membership of a distributor user group which is responsible for supplier/distributor liaison.

TRAFFIC-BUILDING PROGRAMMES

Marketing support must build high levels of traffic through a local network. Local outlets do not have the resources to run sustained corporate campaigns to build the reputation of their outlets and attract customers. They depend on promotions and advertising campaigns that will generate a high level of enquiries all year round. By putting customers in contact with local outlets, the supplier puts the onus on the local outlet to stock the right products at the right price and offer the right level of service. Local outlets want to know that suppliers will support the outlet with campaigns that will generate high levels of traffic.

When a local outlet changes from being a stockist of, say, replacement parts and becomes a retail outlet attracting customers who make impulse purchases rather than just collect orders, the change needs to be accompanied by a programme of regional advertising to attract customers into the branch.

Seasonal consumer offers

National offers for car dealers, such as the summer promotions that coincide with new registration dates, help to generate showroom traffic and provide the salesforce with leads to follow up. Here car manufacturers make a special offer such as free entry in a prize draw or the offer of a free gift on visiting the showroom to attract prospects in the peak buying periods of July/August when the registration changes.

Business-to-business leads

In the business-to-business sector, the offer of a free copy of an authoritative report can help to provide qualified leads for many different types of professional service or product – 'Electrical Safety and Computers', 'Better Parts Stockholding', 'Benefits of Planned Maintenance'. The enquiries these offers generate can be used for follow-up by local outlets and can help to increase volumes of business.

LOYALTY PROGRAMMES

Although few local outlets appear to realise it, customer loyalty is one of the most important issues they face. They need to retain their customers in the face of fierce price competition and they need to sell them an expanding range of products and services so that the business grows naturally. Local outlets are looking for campaigns and programmes that keep customers coming back. This is a particular problem if they are distributing commodity products which are price sensitive. How can they weaken the price argument and show that customers will get a better overall package by dealing with them?

Loyalty programmes can be as simple as promotions to encourage repeat purchase – 10 per cent off your next purchase, volume discounts, rebates for purchase levels, awards for achieving purchasing targets – or they can be integrated with customer satisfaction programmes such as customer care, convenience programmes and contact programmes which keep customers coming back for the higher level of service.

Storecards, for example, have been used widely to build customer loyalty to a retail group and to individual outlets. Despite the apparently high cost of credit, customers have used them for both large and small purchases, providing the outlets with high levels of repeat business. The storecards can also be used to offer account holders privileged services such as special discounts, seasonal offers, or invitations to account holders' social events. They enable the retailer and the local outlet to maintain regular contact with the customer and to build a valuable profile of the account holder as the basis of future marketing activities.

SALES INCENTIVES

Local outlets don't just want to incentivise their customers to buy, they need their own incentive to maintain high levels of business. Incentive schemes should be structured to reward sales effort over the short and long term so that their sales teams put in the right level of effort. There is a broad range of incentive schemes and these are described in more detail in Chapter 10, 'Building sales'.

RECOGNITION PROGRAMMES

Closely related to these are recognition programmes. Local outlets are asked to participate in business development and customer satisfaction programmes and they want to know that their staff will be rewarded for their efforts. Recognition programmes can be a powerful motivating factor in building improved performance within a dealership and they are vital to future development. Recognition programmes are described in more detail in Chapter 9, 'Focusing on customer care'.

SIMPLE PROGRAMME ADMINISTRATION

Marketing programmes can be complex and time consuming to administer, with participation forms, reporting mechanisms, queries on complex programmes, audits and claims. This can act as a barrier to the local outlet, preventing it from gaining the full business benefit from the programme. Local outlets want programmes that are simple to operate and understand so that they can put them to immediate use and benefit from them. These can take several forms:

- development of a simple, easy-to-use operating guide;
- clear examples of programme operation;

- availability of a hotline to handle programme queries;
- simple procedures for dealing with queries.

PRESENTING TO THE LOCAL MANAGEMENT TEAM

This chapter has outlined important aspects of local marketing from the point of view of the local outlet. It is essential that you reflect this in planning and presenting your local support programme.

There are a number of opportunities to present the support programme to local outlets:

- at a national conference as part of an annual review;
- at a regional business meeting;
- at the local outlet;
- in a publication, direct to the local outlet.

The choice of route depends on whether you are presenting a programme that is standard to the whole network or customised to individual outlets. You may also be recruiting new outlets and that will change the emphasis in the presentation. Your presentation should be aimed at the local senior management team and that could determine who presents. A sales representative may handle day-to-day contact with the local outlet, but may not have the experience or the ability to present complex business arguments to senior managers. The benefits of your support programme may be wasted if the presentation is delivered at the wrong level or if the presenter is unable to deal with the management team's questions.

SUMMARY

This chapter has helped you to focus on the type of support the local outlet is looking for. Although you will be developing a programme to meet your own business objectives, you can work in partnership with your local outlets to develop a programme that benefits both parties. The chapter helps you to look at marketing support programmes from the point of view of the outlets – what they want from the relationship with the supplier. Products that offer broad market coverage and fast-moving products will help them to build their business. To sell your products professionally, they need comprehensive product information. A clear statement of corporate direction, together with regular, up-to-date information on company developments will ensure that local outlets understand your business and can plan change in their business to meet your changing requirements. The chapter stresses the importance of regular contact with local outlets and shows how technical support and comprehensive training and development programmes will help them improve the performance of their business in partnership with you. Local outlets expect you to provide effective national marketing support to build their business and they want the means to provide their own local input to marketing programmes. The chapter outlines the different types of support that help the local outlet to build its business – traffic building programmes, customer loyalty programmes, sales incentives and recognition programmes. Most important, it shows how marketing programmes should be simple to administer. Finally, the chapter outlines different options for presenting the support programme to a local management team as part of a continuing relationship or to attract new outlets.

ACTION CHECKLIST

BROAD MARKET COVERAGE

Do your products provide your local outlets with market coverage?

Can they obtain all their products from a single source?

Could you rationalise your range and still provide market coverage?

Does the level of market coverage vary in international markets?

Do you have product variants to meet international market requirements?

Do your products provide outlets with new market opportunities?

Are your products a good fit with the outlet's customer profile?

FAST-MOVING PRODUCTS

Are your products fast moving or do they need high levels of support to improve turnover?

Can you rationalise your range to improve turnover?

Can you introduce impulse products into your current range to stimulate store traffic?

Can you stimulate sales of services by changing the way they are sold or delivered?

Can you break service products into modules to improve turnover?

PRODUCT INFORMATION

What sort of product information do you supply?

How is the information used?

Does the local salesforce need high levels of product knowledge?

How rapidly does product information change and how easily can you update your sales information?

Is your product information sufficiently comprehensive to meet the needs of new sales territories in international markets?

Can you use new technology to make updating easily?

How well do local outlets use product information at the point of sale?

CORPORATE DIRECTION

How well do you communicate your corporate direction?

Are your local outlets aware of your mission statement?

Are there any changes in direction that are likely to impact on your network?

Is your company known in international markets?

Do you share your future plans with your local network?

How easy is it for outsiders to understand your organisation?

Do you keep your network up to date with organisational change?

COMPANY DEVELOPMENTS

Do you publish your financial results to your local outlets?

Have you got a formal system for updating local outlets on technical or marketing changes?

Do you hold regular meetings with your local management teams?

CONTACT

Do you have a contact strategy for your local outlets?

How do you handle day-to-day enquiries?

Are your international teams in regular contact with head office and with each other?

Have you got a member of staff responsible for the quality of contact with local outlets?

Do you have the resources to maintain a high level of contact with international outlets?

Do you have staff located in the territory throughout your international market?

Could your staff use the telephone to improve the frequency of contact?

Are your staff in contact at the right level with your local outlets?

TECHNICAL SUPPORT

How important is technical support to your network?

Do you have a formal system for issuing technical information to the network?

What is the local level of technical skill in your international markets?

Can you use new technology to ensure that up-to-date technical information is available in the local outlets?

TRAINING AND DEVELOPMENT

Is your training accessible or could you introduce more convenient methods of training?

How could you handle training on an international level?

Do training requirements vary in international markets?

Is your training relevant to the needs of your local outlets?

Are local outlets aware of the importance of training?

NATIONAL MARKETING SUPPORT

Does your national advertising help to brand your local outlets?

Is your national and local advertising fully integrated?

Can your standard marketing support programmes be used in all your international territories?

Does your national advertising encourage customers to contact local outlets?

LOCAL INPUT

Do you encourage your local outlets to participate in developing marketing programmes?

Would participation help to make the programmes more acceptable?

How could you make participation work in practical terms?

Do national sales companies develop their own support programmes or can they participate in international programmes?

TRAFFIC BUILDING

How much effort do you put into building local customer traffic?

Can you introduce new promotional offers to increase traffic?

CUSTOMER LOYALTY

Are your local outlets aware of the importance of customer loyalty?

What is the level of repeat business in local outlets?

What type of programmes could you introduce to improve customer loyalty?

Do customer expectations vary across international markets?

SALES INCENTIVES

Do your sales incentives encourage the right balance between long- and short-term objectives?

RECOGNITION PROGRAMMES

Do you operate recognition schemes for programmes that are strategically important, such as customer satisfaction programmes?

SIMPLE PROGRAMME ADMINISTRATION

Are your business and marketing programmes easy to operate?

Can you simplify administrative procedures in any way?

4

ASSESSING MARKET OPPORTUNITIES

INTRODUCTION

The previous chapter explained how the supplier should take the local outlet's point of view in presenting the franchise opportunities to a local management team. This chapter explains how suppliers and local outlets can work together to assess opportunities in the local market. The information that derives from this assessment is used to develop a local marketing plan which in turn provides the input for the support programme. The theme of this book is that local markets should not be treated as scaled-down versions of the national market: they have their own unique characteristics and the local market assessment should reflect this. The chapter covers the key steps needed to achieve this.

NATIONAL RESEARCH

The programme begins with national research into a number of key areas.

- What do customers want from the your local network?
- How do they perceive your outlets compared with your competitors?
- What improvements would they like?
- Where are the greatest opportunities for growing the business?
- What is the potential for the local outlet when it is fully operational?

The research is concentrated on two main areas – customer requirements and the market for local services. Larger organisations may have their own research departments in-house to handle this type of work, but typically it is probably more cost effective to sub-contract the work to specialist research companies that can offer an independent viewpoint and provide a professional service tailored to your needs. In interviewing customers and prospects, the research company would select locations where the supplier had an outlet and where competitors were located. It should then evaluate customer perceptions and requirements against current distributor communications to see whether perception was influenced by them. This type of customer research can also be used to assess the variation in perception by market sector.

A computer environmental services company carried out telephone research into the buying patterns of major public and private companies that operated regional offices. It wanted to find out whether the local office purchased its services autonomously or whether it was controlled by central purchasing decisions. The research indicated a fairly even split between central and local purchases, but further research indicated that local branches that could buy autonomously preferred to deal with substantial organisations with a national reputation for quality, rather than small local companies. The computer services company was able to encourage its distributors and local branches to present themselves as members of a national group that was able to offer a local service. The growth opportunities would come if it was able to replicate the same high standards throughout its network and offer multi-site customers a consistent standard.

Research like this can also help to identify the locations where the greatest opportunity for growth would come. A number of companies offer a special site evaluation service which provides a complete profile of a branch's market with computerised assessment of the demographic profile and other factors.

Research into site location and the selection of distributors is outside the scope of this book, but is covered in Vinoo Iyer's book, *Managing and Motivating Your Agents and Distributors*, also in the Pitman Financial Times series.

LOCAL RESEARCH

This initial process enables suppliers to pinpoint sites with the greatest potential for growth and development. Local research is perhaps a misnomer because local could mean a whole country or an entire continent rather than just a town, but the principle is the same – to identify locations where the greatest number of customers are looking for a service that matches the profile of the service available through the distributor network.

Research by the supplier can be used to identify what kind of service is currently available in the location and compare it with the quality of service that customers are demanding. In the analysis, the supplier would assess the current performance of any distributor that was already operating there and compare it with competitive performance or an established internal benchmark.

The supplier's local research can be complemented by research carried out by the local outlet. While local outlets may not have the sophisticated research facilities enjoyed by larger companies, they are very close to their customers and they possess a great deal of local knowledge. Local outlets have the detailed understanding of local customers and competitors that enables them to fine-tune a service to local conditions. Putting the two sources of information together can provide a detailed profile which gives a basis for decision making. The supplier understands national marketing trends and is aware of the strengths and weaknesses of his organisation's performance. The local outlet interprets that understanding at local level.

To help local outlets carry out their research, many suppliers provide a guide to carrying out local research which describes sources of information, including:

- telephone surveys of customers and prospects;
- monitoring local press, radio and television for details of competitive advertising;
- anonymous visits to competitive outlets;
- price monitoring;
- discussions with customers and prospects at local focus groups and social events;

- using salesforce reports to identify buying patterns in the market;
- using special offers and special events to capture information on customers and prospects;
- using business surveys and commercial sources to provide general research information;
- using the services of specialist retail-research companies.

SUCCESS FACTORS

The information that is available through research can be used to identify the factors needed to succeed in the local market. Will it take:

- a wider product range?
- better quality of service?
- faster delivery?
- longer opening hours?
- better location?
- lower prices?
- better overall performance or any other combination of services?

Compare two hotels – one a long-established local private hotel which has strong links with the community. It hosts meetings of the local Round Table and many other social and business groups, and is a well-recognised private hotel for visitors. Although it is situated near a major business centre, it does not cater specifically for business travellers. An international hotel chain spots the business travel potential through research and investigates the potential and the opportunities needed to succeed. The hotel group profiles a package which includes complementary travel from the local airport or rail station, car-hire facilities within the hotel complex, a brand name and reputation that business travellers trust, credit-card facilities and a business centre with fax, telephone, photocopier, and meeting rooms that visitors can hire. On the other hand, it lacks the personal service, tradition and atmosphere of the older local hotel. If another hotel group was to acquire the older hotel, how would it assess its long-term potential? Each of the hotels has its own inherent success factors but they offer different solutions to the same problem.

ASSESSING THE DISTRIBUTOR PROFILE

By assessing the success factors needed in the local market, the supplier can also evaluate the performance of the local outlet and determine the level of support needed for it to succeed. Chapter 9, 'Focusing on the customer', explains how to help local outlets meet high standards of customer care. By evaluating each of the success factors in turn, the supplier can work out the support that is required to achieve success in that market. The decision then becomes an investment decision – if the supplier provides a support package costing £x, the local outlet is likely to build additional revenue and profit worth £y. If the package also provides other benefits in terms of winning strategic business or improving levels of customer loyalty, the investment may be more attractive. The same principles can be applied to competitors – how well does their profile match the local success factors?

Take a firm of solicitors. An established local practice in a community situated near a new motorway with growing business parks and access to Europe has worked with most of the established businesses in the town and sees an increase in business as new companies move in. A regional group of solicitors identifies an opportunity and sets up offices in the area. Its pitch to the local business community is that the new office will be staffed by solicitors experienced in business administration and in European legislation. They have tailored their service more precisely to the needs of the community. While each practice offers the same basic legal service, the newer office has an immediate competitive advantage.

LOCAL FOCUS GROUPS

Customers can help to determine the shape of the local business by participating in focus groups. A focus group is a group of customers or prospects who are invited to an event and asked to give their views on a product, a service or an organisation. A discussion leader, who is normally independent, guides the discussion and records the comments of the participants. Although the discussion is structured, it also gives participants the opportunity to comment on any aspect of the business. Focus groups can help to confirm ideas thrown up by research and to steer the company towards making decisions and they can help to gauge the response to an offer.

Companies who have run local focus groups as a means of assessing market and product operations have been surprised that customers have enjoyed talking about work so much, and have continued the practice of arranging meetings for local customers as a means of maintaining regular informal contact with the market.

A European vehicle-refinishing supplier ran a series of focus groups around the country to gauge distributor and customer reactions to a new colour identification system. The new colour identification system would offer customers important productivity benefits, improve colour accuracy and make updating simpler. However, because of the cost of providing information in the new format, the manufacturer would have to make a charge for a service that had previously been supplied free. The focus group tackled the issue of charging and tried to establish how much customers would be willing to pay for such a service. The focus groups gave the manufacturer a useful insight into potential customer reactions to the colour information service, but also highlighted a latent opportunity to arrange social events for customers. Most of the customers who attended the focus group agreed that they found social events like this a useful forum for informal discussions on business. As a result, the manufacturer allocated part of his local support budget to funding a series of social events run by local distributors. This helped distributors to improve relations with customers and provided useful insight into local market needs.

KEY DIFFERENTIATORS

Local research and assessment should provide a list of success factors that local outlets will need to achieve, plus a means of differentiating your network's offer from competitors. The key differentiators are what gives the outlet the competitive edge – the solicitor with the European business experience, or the hotel with its specialist service for business travellers. Both they and their competitors met the criteria for successful operation, but what distinguished them in the business sector was the business package.

DEVELOPING A SUPPORT PACKAGE

Success is not built just on specific differentiators, it depends on a whole package of skills, special offers, prices, services, products and related services, and the analysis of local market opportunities will help suppliers and local outlets to focus on all the factors that are important to success. Chapter 6 on 'Assessing support requirements', describes this in more detail.

TEST MARKETING

Careful research and joint programmes with local outlets can be useful in determining the right package for the local market, but before a programme is put into national operation, it can be useful to test the concept and evaluate the results in a test market. A limited test using a variety of support options provides an opportunity to measure the results of different approaches and to adjust tactics before the national launch.

Consumer test markets

Consumer-goods manufacturers make regular use of test markets aligned to commercial television regions to assess the potential of new products or promotional strategies. The television companies provide research data on the demographic and marketing characteristics of their territory and manufacturers use this to supplement their own market research. In selecting sites for new retail outlets, the availability of advertising can be a strong determining factor and manufacturers use the test-marketing facilities to evaluate the potential returns from advertising. A region is chosen whose characteristics are as close to possible to the national market profile and sales of the product or outlet are measured over a period of time with different levels of advertising and promotional support. If the test is successful, the manufacturer then has the information and the confidence to develop a national plan.

Pilot programmes

Pilot programmes are similar to test markets except that an entire programme is put on test rather than just a product. If, for example, a company wanted to launch a new range of outlets or a new concept in distribution it would set up a pilot operation in a test market to evaluate the feasibility of operating and marketing programmes and to test the response of staff and customers. A pilot programme is a full-scale version of the whole programme except that the company is taking a limited financial risk. The programme would be fully researched and checked against a list of key success factors to see whether it would work.

The pilot programme could be used by a smaller, regionally-based distributor network to evaluate a number of possible strategies:

- opening new branches outside the region;
- introducing new types of service within the region.

At international level it could be used to:

- evaluate market potential in new territories;
- restructure an organisation.

A pilot programme can be a useful way of measuring the opportunities in a new market, but it can provide a false perspective if the results are not measured accurately.

ASSESSING PROMOTIONAL IMPACT

Provided a company has sophisticated control systems it can carry out evaluations of the impact of different promotional strategies. By adjusting the mix or weight of promotional strategies and measuring the change in sales across different outlets, a supplier can determine the optimum support strategy for the whole network and for different outlets within the network. Breweries, for example, use the computerised network reporting systems to assess promotional response by region or by individual outlet.

SUMMARY

This chapter outlines the type of research that should be carried out as a basis for planning local support programmes. It explains how local outlets are in the best position to understand their customers and their local markets, but local research must be integrated with information from national research programmes. The chapter describes how suppliers can provide their local outlets with suitable data and help them carry out their research in a professional way. Research helps both parties to determine the success factors for local marketing and provides a basis for assessing the distributor profile and identifying the key differentiators that need to be addressed in developing a support package. The chapter shows how test marketing, pilot programmes and promotional response tracking can be used to evaluate the potential impact of different marketing strategies.

ACTION CHECKLIST

NATIONAL RESEARCH

How relevant is your national research to local market conditions?

Does your national research identify buying patterns that might influence the prospects of your local outlets?

Does your national research reflect patterns in international markets?

Do you conduct national market research for each of your international territories?

LOCAL RESEARCH

Are your local outlets equipped to carry out research?

Can you supplement their efforts with professional research support?

Do you provide them with guidelines on obtaining research data?

Do your corporate information systems provide useful local research data?

Can you use focus groups to improve your understanding of the local market?

SUCCESS FACTORS

What local success factors are identified by your research?

How do the success factors vary across international markets?

Do your current support programmes enable you to improve those success factors?

What are the key differentiators between your outlets and those of competitors?

DISTRIBUTOR PROFILE

Does research enable you to evaluate the potential of your local outlets?

Is an investment in local support likely to provide you with useful business benefits?

ASSESSING PROMOTIONAL IMPACT

Can you use research results to fine-tune your support package?

Do you use test marketing to evaluate the impact of support packages?

Can you use test-market facilities in your international markets?

Do your corporate information systems enable you to assess the impact of different support strategies?

5

DEVELOPING A LOCAL MARKETING PLAN

INTRODUCTION

Planning is the key to success in any business activity and effective local marketing depends on the successful co-ordination and integration of a series of individual marketing plans. The local marketing plan shows the supplier team that the local management team has given full consideration to its proposals for dealing with challenges in the local market and also shows it is fully aware of the support that is available to help it meet its local needs. This example of a local marketing plan is based on a car dealership, but the principles could be applied to any type of outlet.

The plan covers the following key areas:

- overall objectives;
- SWOT analysis;
- market sectors;
- competitive activity;
- market-sector activities;
- customer focus standards;
- customer-satisfaction objectives;
- developing skills;
- salesforce actions;
- generating enquiries;
- customer incentives;
- customer-loyalty actions;
- advertising;
- direct mail;

- special campaigns;
- joint promotions;
- wholesale activities;
- sales-incentive programmes;
- new technology;
- perceived position.

OVERALL OBJECTIVES

It is essential that local outlets realise the importance of setting overall objectives; many are concerned with tactical promotions which provide short-term gains, but do not consider the activities within the context of overall objectives. Within a car dealership, for example, the overall objective might be seen as selling x cars per year, but there are other objectives that may be more important. Ensuring the highest level of customer satisfaction throughout a dealership, for example, would ensure that dealers paid attention to every aspect of their activities. This would not only impact on new car sales, but would ensure that customers made full use of the parts and service operations and continued to use the dealership throughout their ownership of the car. Provided they are satisfied with the standard of service they receive throughout the ownership of the car, they will be likely to give both the manufacturer and the dealership serious consideration when they come to choose their next car.

By setting key objectives that reflect overall objectives aimed at raising long-term customer satisfaction, the dealer will operate a balanced series of programmes and provide the right level of resources to each department that impacts on customer satisfaction. The overall objective could be restated to:

- 'sell x cars by ensuring the highest levels of customer satisfaction';
- a second objective could be 'to maximise profit and return on investment by operating efficiently and cost effectively without affecting levels of customer satisfaction'.

The individual dealers' objectives must also be integrated with the manufacturer's objectives. Again these are likely to be linked to achieving the highest levels of customer satisfaction, but there may be other strategic activities such as achieving market leadership in the high-volume car market or building an effective aftermarket operation to ensure long-term success.

SWOT ANALYSIS

This is an effective way of helping local outlets to analyse critically their own activities.

- Do their facilities match the operating standards and customer-focus standards set by the manufacturer?
- Have they got key strengths in the important sectors of the market?
- Where can they make the greatest improvements in line with their business objectives?
- Do they have the skills to meet current and future objectives?
- Are they making the most of the opportunities to build on their specific strengths?

In carrying out the SWOT analysis, local outlets should analyse each of the activities that are covered in the remainder of this marketing plan and draw up a prioritised list of essential actions to improve the key performance factors. The distributor specialist should then work through the analysis to determine the levels of support needed to ensure success.

IDENTIFYING KEY MARKET SECTORS

The SWOT analysis can be applied to the whole local market and also to specific market sectors. By analysing the different sectors of their market, local outlets can be more precise in their planning and can set out a number of specific objectives which can be achieved more easily. For a car dealer there are a number of competitive market sectors:

- new-car sales to domestic users;
- second-car sales to domestic users;

- business/executive car sales;
- small fleet sales;
- fleet sales that are often handled by the manufacturer;
- used-car sales;
- commercial vehicle (new and used) sales;
- wholesale activities;
- sales of special vehicles such as high-performance cars;
- motability sales;
- parts and service sales;
- bodyshop sales.

The aftermarket activities can also be divided into further sectors:

- scheduled servicing;
- replacement parts for DIY motorists;
- wholesale parts operations;
- accessory sales;
- repairs;
- seasonal service and parts sales.

By looking at each of these individually, dealers can also assess where they will get the best return on their investment or where they need to take the strongest actions to deal with competitive activity. Dealing with opportunities on a sector basis also ensures that individual staff have achievable targets which can be precisely monitored.

COMPETITIVE ACTIVITY

This section of the marketing plan is a crucial element in developing a local marketing plan. While other elements of marketing support can be customised from national programmes, the levels of competition are unique to each market. In the marketing plan, local outlets should evaluate the strengths of local competitors.

- What market share do they have and who are they?
- Which customers are they dealing with?
- What are their pricing levels?
- What sort of package are they offering their customers?

- What is their promotional activity?
- Why do customers prefer their products?
- What actions does the dealer plan to take to win back business from competition?

This analysis of competitive activity focuses the local team's attention on marketing factors that may prevent it from reaching its full potential. It should not only concentrate on winning back lost business, but also on strengthening its relationships with customers who might be influenced by competitive activity. Local outlets should identify how they intend to monitor competitive activity and how they will respond to different types of competitive threat.

MARKET SECTOR ACTIVITIES

The market-sector analysis helps to define the key tasks in each sector. The marketing plan should now describe the main activities in each sector in precise terms.

- To boost new-car sales to domestic users, we will appoint an additional salesperson, increase advertising spending by 15 per cent and introduce a new computerised prospecting system to support the sales effort. Customers will be offered seasonal incentives at key buying times and we will introduce new pre-delivery inspection techniques to ensure that the customer hand-over achieves the highest levels of satisfaction.
- In the business/executive car sector, we will be setting up a mailing database and targeting business users with regular information on special offers and updates on business motoring. We will make use of the business drivers' magazine available from the manufacturer and we will appoint a salesperson to take complete responsibility for the business sector.
- In the small fleet sector, we will be offering customers an improved service package which includes overnight service, vehicle collection and delivery, replacement vehicle if theirs is off the road, and a service charge card scheme which fleet drivers can use at other dealers in the network if they break down.

- we are introducing new quality-inspection processes on our used cars and offering more competitive warranties with specific long-term service offers for customers who buy cars with extended warranties;
- to regain our share of the scheduled service market from independent service outlets, we are offering a new menu-priced modular service agreement which will make customers feel more confident about the price they pay;
- we aim to increase our wholesale parts business by offering customers an overnight delivery service plus a whole range of incentive offers to encourage volume purchase;
- our bodyshop service has recently been upgraded and we will make presentations to a number of insurance groups so that we can obtain their approval as authorised repair centres;
- in general terms, we will be aiming to improve our customer satisfaction ratings for the entire dealership by carrying out the following customer focus activities.

This is a range of specialist activities that can each be measured and monitored. As well as increasing sales, many of the activities have built-in customer service features that help the local outlet to meet overall objectives. These activities are not vague intentions but specific actions, which can be delegated and produce measurable results. Some of the actions are described in more detail later in the chapter.

CUSTOMER FOCUS STANDARDS

Customer focus standards are described in detail in Chapter 9 – 'Focusing on the customer'; they are equivalent to operating standards but cover factors such as convenience, quality of service and customer care which have a direct impact on customer satisfaction levels. There are also customer satisfaction programmes which aim to improve the overall performance.

Again, these should be described in terms of specific measurable activities, rather than intentions to improve performance:

- we are introducing longer opening hours so that more customers can visit us when it suits them, in the evenings or at weekends;
- we are increasing the number of customer parking spaces to improve convenience;
- we will be training staff to provide additional cover at reception peak times so that we can reduce customer waiting times;
- we are automating our cost and control systems so that we can produce invoices more quickly and accurately;
- we are providing customers with a hotline number manned by a specialist in customer relations so that people feel we can deal with their queries fairly and promptly;
- we are introducing charge cards for our regular customers to improve convenience and make it quicker and easier for them to deal with us;
- we will install a dedicated fax line for our parts wholesale customers to make it easier for them to order.

CUSTOMER SATISFACTION OBJECTIVES

Customer satisfaction levels are measured by the results of customer questionnaires on their satisfaction with different aspects of local performance. Most questionnaires consist of large numbers of questions to give a complete picture of the local outlet, but there are several key areas that have the highest impact on customer satisfaction. The overall aim is to raise satisfaction levels from previous years, so if the index showed a rating of say, 75 per cent, the local outlet might aim for a rating of say, 80 per cent in the coming year. However, to achieve this, it needs to take special action or operate programmes that will improve satisfaction levels. The customer focus standards provide a sound base but activities such as introducing a courtesy car programme will help to improve customer convenience and satisfaction. These are examples of actions identified by car manufacturers as being crucial to satisfaction:

- improve new vehicle inspection procedures before delivery to customers so that there are no irritating faults in the crucial first stage of ownership;
- improve service department standards so that customers continue to return to the dealership throughout the period of ownership;
- set up a procedure for dealing with urgent customer complaints as soon as they are identified through the questionnaire.

DEVELOPING SKILLS

Skilled staff are the key to running an efficient business and delivering the highest standards of customer care. The marketing plan should show how local outlets intend to develop the skills of their key staff and how they intend to make use of the training programmes that are available. The skills analysis described in Chapter 6, 'Assessing support requirements', will help to identify the skills needed to meet business objectives and the section on training in Chapter 8, 'Achieving consistent standards', provides a number of different options for developing skills at local level. The marketing plan should show how those skills developments relate to achieving key objectives:

- we will enrol recently-recruited sales staff on the customer care programme to improve their customer handling skills;
- our service receptionists are participating in the advanced receptionist's course to improve their technical and customer-handling skills;
- we will enrol one of the senior sales executives on the fleet marketing programme to improve penetration in the business sector;
- the dealership senior management team will participate in the seminars on strategic business development for the 90s;
- we will be taking part in the on-site retail development programmes that are offered from the end of the year;
- we will continue to encourage all members of staff to improve their skills by participating in relevant programmes;

- we will appoint a training specialist to co-ordinate training within the dealership to ensure we meet both operating and marketing requirements.

SALESFORCE ACTIONS

The performance of the salesforce has traditionally been seen as integral to the success of the local outlet. New-car sales are still fundamental to the whole dealership operation and actions to improve performance in this area will make a significant difference. Look at the organisation of the salesforce, the number of people, the support they get from members of staff, the support programmes they have available to develop business and the infrastructure that supports them. Many car dealers are also looking at ways of bringing the sales and other departments within the dealership into closer working relationships so that they can work more effectively as a team:

- we are appointing a new salesperson and we will be giving members of the salesforce individual responsibility for improving performance in key market sectors. This individual responsibility will enable each member of the team to concentrate on one sector rather than duplicating effort in some areas and leaving others undeveloped;
- we are forming project teams from parts and service departments to work with the sales team on developing integrated offers to new- and used-car customers;
- we are introducing new database-management methods so that we can handle prospects and follow-up more efficiently and take full advantage of the company marketing programmes available;
- we will be making use of the national new-car-sales prospect register to supplement our local information.

GENERATING ENQUIRIES

No matter how efficient the salesforce, it cannot improve perform-ance if it is not getting the right level of enquiries. The local outlet needs to show how it will attract customers to the showroom or generate enquiries through advertisements, traffic-building pro-motions or other incentives to enquire or buy:

- we will mail all car and service customers whose cars are reaching the end of the second or third year of ownership, the most popular time for changing a vehicle;
- we will run a high-profile local advertising campaign to point out the value of our part-exchange offers and to show the range of prices and products on offer;
- we will run a series of themed competition offers to encourage enquiries;
- we will hold a series of special events for fleet prospects and customers to explain our changing service and range of business offers available;
- we will utilise the national advertising campaigns and response service to build up lists of prospects in our territory;
- we will be offering test drives to business prospects from their own premises.

These methods of generating enquiries operate at a general level, as well as in specific marketing sectors.

CUSTOMER INCENTIVES

The other areas on the marketing plan are specific activities that tend to overlap with the more general activities described in the first part of this chapter. They are repeated so that local outlets do not over-look the support that is available to them. Customer incentives are an integral part of the sales process designed to make customers move towards purchase:

- we will use the new-registration summer competition to encourage a high level of showroom traffic during the key months of July and August;

- we will make a number of offers that entitle customers to prize draws for purchasing by a certain date;
- we will be offering customers free safety checks to generate higher levels of parts and service business;
- we will be offering reduced-price accessories to improve sales of our new range of leisure vehicles;
- we will be developing a planned programme of customer incentives for each of the key market sectors.

CUSTOMER LOYALTY ACTIONS

As well as running incentive competitions to attract new customers and prospects, local outlets must concentrate on retaining those customers and building higher levels of repeat business. In the example of the car dealer, customer loyalty programmes are designed to keep customers in contact with the dealership throughout the ownership period so that they hold a positive attitude when they are considering their next purchase. However, when local outlets are handling faster-moving products they need to build frequency of purchase, and the emphasis within the programme shifts:

- new car customers will be invited to visit the parts and service departments so that they are aware of the full scope of dealership service;
- we will offer customers vouchers giving discounts on first year servicing with the offer of special gifts if they sign up for an optional extended warranty;
- we will maintain regular contact with customers by inviting them to regular events and sending out details of regular offers;
- we will encourage more frequent parts purchase by offering volume discounts and other price-off-next-purchase offers;
- we will reward loyal service customers with the offer of free checks and the use of a courtesy vehicle when their car is off the road;
- we will offer business users exclusive membership of a business

drivers club which includes special offers and arrangements for quick service and preferential treatment.

ADVERTISING

Advertisements are used across many of the marketing activities described earlier. Local outlets have the option of developing their own campaigns or making use of material supplied by the manufacturer. Many suppliers ask local outlets to include budgets based on a percentage of their target turnover and ask them to run advertisements at certain frequencies during the year. The local marketing plan should include the following tasks:

- we will develop a corporate advertisement to build the reputation of the dealership for providing a complete service to motorists;
- we will develop a standard format for making special offers throughout the year;
- we will plan a media schedule to show when the advertisements will appear and relate them to key events such as new registration, model launches, motor shows and other national events;
- we will run a series of advertisements to promote priced parts and service offers;
- we will develop local radio commercials to raise the profile of our regional dealer group;
- we will use the dealer advertising service to book our media space and take advantage of volume discounts;
- we will use the dealer advertising rebate to make better use of our advertising budget;
- we will set up a telephone response unit to deal promptly with enquiries from advertisements;
- we will develop special advertisements to improve awareness in each of the key market sectors;
- we will allocate budgets to reflect the balance between market sectors.

DIRECT MAIL

Local outlets can use direct mail to make their marketing more precise and measurable. The key to good direct mail is a well-organised database, and part of the marketing plan must be focused on building that database:

- we will record all enquiries in the showroom, over the telephone or in response to advertisements or other offers;
- we will make special offers or run events to generate enquiries and names of prospects;
- we will use names and addresses from national advertising campaigns to develop a local database;
- we will ensure that the database is kept up to date by telephone checking;
- we will use the services of a database-management agency.

Direct mail should be used selectively to achieve specific business objectives. In the marketing plan, local outlets should identify how they will use direct mail and how they will evaluate programme results:

- we will use direct mail to reach car owners reaching the end of their second or third year of ownership;
- we will mail all business users with details of the new business users club;
- we will mail local authority drivers with details of special schemes for civil service drivers;
- we will mail wholesale customers with details of seasonal and other promotional offers;
- we will aim at a 2 per cent response rate;
- we will follow up the mailing programme with telephone contact.

This ensures that local outlets use direct mail in a targeted way, rather than just sending out letters in a vague fashion.

SPECIAL CAMPAIGNS

Special campaigns are used to support special events such as the launch of a new product or some special offers that fall outside the scope of normal marketing support activities. A new product launch is a major event that is critical to the success of both supplier and local outlet, and it requires considerable effort to make the most of the launch opportunity. Local outlets must be aware of their full responsibility for the launch and take all the actions needed for success. This marketing plan includes just a few of the activities that would be included in a launch guide:

- we will set up a launch team to co-ordinate the launch programme and delegate responsibility for key actions;
- we will develop a dealership timetable based on the sample provided in the launch guide;
- we will order and use launch-support material described in the guide;
- we will prepare advertisements and direct mail to communicate the new product to key prospects;
- we will develop a sales and marketing plan to cover the pre-launch, launch and post-launch period;
- we will discuss the launch programme with your distributor representative.

JOINT PROMOTIONS

Local outlets may co-operate with each other to improve the impact of their programmes and to strengthen the brand image of the entire network. For example, a group of regional outlets such as Southern Vauxhall dealers or Thames Ford dealers might run a joint campaign. Promotions like this are designed to raise awareness of the whole group or to make special offers run by all members of the group.

- we will develop a programme with other regional distributors for promoting special offers;
- we will agree contributions to the joint marketing programme;

- we will provide details to be included in the joint communications;
- we will agree how enquiries and sales should be handled and allocated between participating dealers.

WHOLESALE ACTIVITIES

Wholesaling is an increasingly important activity as local outlets realise that the service they offer to customers they can also offer to other retail outlets, provided they are not direct competitors.

Here the outlet uses its buying power and organisational skills to act as a secondary distributor and stockholder for the manufacturer. The key marketing activities must be used to improve the quality of service and make the most of the opportunities:

- we will research the opportunities for wholesale business in different market sectors;
- we will identify the key factors that ensure wholesale success;
- we will develop services such as overnight delivery or volume discounts to encourage higher levels of purchase;
- we will use promotional material to improve understanding and awareness of the wholesale operation;
- we will appoint a wholesale specialist to co-ordinate the programme;
- we will set up efficient order-taking and order-processing facilities to capture business efficiently;
- we will develop and operate direct marketing programmes to reach key targets.

SALES-INCENTIVE PROGRAMMES

Sales-incentive programmes will help to maintain the levels of motivation and interest in building sales. Local outlets should show how they intend to use the incentive programmes to reach key targets in each market sector. Incentive programmes can be used in an ad-hoc way to boost the level of overall sales but they can also be used in a structured way to achieve key marketing objectives:

- we will set sales incentive targets for overall sales performance;
- we will include incentives for participation in training programmes and other business development programmes;
- we will operate structured incentive programmes that encourage new business development and customer loyalty;
- we will operate recognition and incentive programmes linked to the key customer satisfaction indicators so that non-sales staff are rewarded for their contribution to overall dealership performance;
- we will participate in the manufacturer's incentive programmes which reward the whole dealership for achievement in essential areas;
- we will participate in national competition and award schemes against other distributors.

USING NEW TECHNOLOGY

New technology can be a valuable aid to marketing and local outlets should be encouraged to make use of it. It can help to improve the quality of customer service by providing better information, freeing staff for customer service duties and providing administrative support for marketing programmes. For example, a service information database can provide up-to-date service information for instant diagnosis on individual customer vehicles and automate procedures for managing service operations. The key tasks in the marketing plan might include:

- we will implement the service database and train staff in its use;
- we will utilise the database to improve the efficiency of service management;
- we will use the administrative software to speed up back-office activities and free staff for customer contact duties;
- we will utilise the dealer interactive video system to train staff in product knowledge and to offer customers choice at the point of sale.

PERCEIVED POSITION

The marketing plan should help the local outlet achieve key marketing objectives and also to develop a planned perception from his customers. The planned perception is the way a customer sees the local outlet – friendly, customer focused, easy to deal with, convenient, flexible. The local outlet should have identified the important perceptions in its assessment of the local marketing opportunities. This planned perception will reflect the important factors that customers are looking for and will help to position the outlet in relation to competitors. The local management team can then measure planned perception against actual perception to see where improvements can be made. This section of the marketing plan is in three parts:

- what are the target perceptions of the dealership?
- how does the dealer fare in each of the sectors?
- what actions are being taken to improve performance in each of the key areas?

REVIEW PROCESS

To help local outlets put together a marketing plan, the supplier needs to prepare a formal planning guide that outlines the key activities to be included and to brief local outlets thoroughly on this. Personal contact from a distributor specialist can help to guide the local management team through the planning process and ensure that the proposals are reviewed carefully and promptly. The planning guide might include:

- marketing plan framework;
- details of the manufacturer's marketing plans;
- working with distributors;
- targets and incentives.

SUMMARY

This example of a marketing plan for a car dealership shows how a structured approach to planning can help local outlets to explore alternative routes to developing their business and ensure that they do not omit any important actions. The most effective plans are expressed in specific, measurable terms and are developed through co-operation between supplier and local outlet. This chapter provides the basis for a local marketing plan which is prepared jointly by the local outlet and the supplier. It goes through each stage of the planning process to show the factors the local outlet should consider. The chapter divides the plan into the following areas: overall objectives, SWOT analysis, identifying key market sectors, competitive activity, market sector activities, customer focus standards, customer satisfaction objectives, developing skills, salesforce actions, generating enquiries, customer incentives, customer loyalty actions, advertising, direct mail, special campaigns, joint promotions, wholesale activities, sales incentive programmes, using new technology, and perceived position. For each factor, the chapter provides a list of actions that might be taken by a fictitious car dealership. Finally, the chapter suggests a review process to ensure that the plan is acceptable to both parties.

ACTION CHECKLIST

OVERALL OBJECTIVES

Are your local outlets' objectives in line with your own business objectives?

If they are not, is there any conflict with or potential impact on your business?

Do overall objectives vary across international territories?

SWOT

Does the SWOT analysis highlight any particular problems or opportunities that require urgent action?

Is the local outlet taking actions on the SWOT analysis?

Is there any recurring pattern in the analyses from other outlets in the network?

MARKET SECTOR ACTIVITY

Are there any significant market sectors in your local business? Does an overall pattern emerge, or does each outlet have its own pattern?

Do market sector patterns vary across international markets?

How would this affect your support policies?

Have the local outlets identified the actions they are taking to improve performance in the important sectors?

Are their activities measurable?

What additional support resources are required to help local outlets to succeed in each of their chosen sectors?

COMPETITIVE ACTIVITY

Do you and your local outlets have plans in place to deal with competitive activity?

CUSTOMER FOCUS

Do your local outlets understand customers' expectations?

Do customer expectations vary across international markets?

Have you established customer focus standards, and are these mandatory on all your outlets?

Are your international customer focus standards aligned to local customer expectations?

What specific, measurable actions are your outlets taking to comply with the standards?

Do you measure customer satisfaction with your local outlets?

Are your customer satisfaction ratings integrated with your customer focus standards?

SKILLS DEVELOPMENT

Do you have a skills profile for each of your outlets?

Is the skills profile used to develop targeted training and development programmes?

Are there any serious gaps in the skills profile which could adversely affect long-term performance?

If you are entering new international territories, are there significant skills gaps to be filled?

SALES ACTIONS

How good is current sales performance in the local outlets?

What sort of support can you provide to improve performance?

Should the emphasis be put on attracting new business or retaining the loyalty of existing customers?

COMMUNICATIONS

Have your local outlets developed specific proposals for advertising and other forms of promotion?

Does national legislation affect your plans for international marketing support programmes?

Do their plans reflect your own marketing and communications objectives?

Are there any special marketing activities that are crucial to long-term success?

Do you provide your local outlets with comprehensive information on operating effective communications programmes?

NEW TECHNOLOGY

Are you planning to introduce new technology to improve the performance of local outlets?

Do you have the skills and resources to implement the new technology successfully?

Are you able to utilise communications technology across international markets?

PARTICIPATION IN PLANNING

Have your local outlets participated fully in the development of the plans?

Do you have a formal review process for the plans?

6

ASSESSING SUPPORT REQUIREMENTS

INTRODUCTION

The marketing plan helps local outlets focus on key actions to meet their overall business objectives. It also enables suppliers to determine whether the local outlet is developing business in the right direction and to assess the level of support needed to meet different objectives. Chapter 7, 'Tailoring marketing programmes', shows how support programmes can be customised to the local needs of different outlets, but this chapter shows how suppliers can assess individual requirements. This is an important stage in fine-tuning marketing support programmes so that they reflect local conditions. To demonstrate how the support programme can be related to business performance, the support requirements will be analysed in the same sequence as the marketing plan.

By looking at support requirements in this way, support can be provided at two levels:

- generic support to ensure that the whole network meets customer satisfaction targets;
- specific support needed to succeed in local markets and make a contribution to the overall success of the network.

SETTING OVERALL OBJECTIVES

As the marketing plan shows, the local outlet will be setting marketing objectives at two levels:

- objectives that enable it to meet the supplier's overall objectives;
- marketing objectives that are related to its own local marketing conditions.

The balance between the two will be determined by the relationship with the supplier:

- a franchised outlet will have a close relationship and is likely to share the same business and marketing objectives;
- a multi-franchise, independent outlet will be reconciling its objectives with those of the supplier.

The franchised outlet is completely dependent on the manufacturer for support, programmes and funding to meet marketing objectives, while the independent outlet selects the support that is appropriate to its overall business and may develop objectives that are contrary to those of the supplier.

The supplier may therefore have to devote part of his support resources to encouraging the outlet to participate in marketing programmes. This process of developing overall objectives requires a clear definition of the supplier's own objectives and staff with the ability to communicate these clearly and effectively to the local management team. The local contact may be a sales representative for day-to-day business, but it may require a member of the supplier's senior management team to convince the local management team that the objectives are worth pursuing.

ASSESSING STRENGTHS AND WEAKNESSES

The SWOT analysis encourages local outlets to look closely at their individual strengths and weaknesses and this can help to tailor precisely programmes and other forms of support to local conditions. The SWOT analysis will help local outlets identify where they need to put more effort into a market sector or where they should try to improve their performance even further. It will help them identify where they need to improve particular skills and what results they can expect. The SWOT analysis provides a very precise guide to support.

DEALING WITH COMPETITIVE ACTIVITY

Support levels will be determined by two factors – how well outlets understand their local competition and the level of competition. Chapter 4, 'Assessing market opportunities', explained how suppliers and local outlets can work together to carry out the research using analysis of local media, 'mystery shopper' visits to competitors' premises and discussions with customers and prospects on competitive activity. It is essential that local outlets get a detailed understanding of local competitors and can relate that to national patterns. If, for example, a competitive chain moves into the area, the supplier team will be able to identify the nature of the competitive threat and will be able to brief the local outlet.

This helps raise the local outlets' awareness of competitive threats, ensuring that they are able to recognise and deal with the threats.

The second level of support helps local outlets to deal with different levels of competitive activity. By analysing in the marketing plan, the nature of the competition, the outlet should be able to work out whether it needs to respond with:

- lower prices;
- better package-deals;
- more-frequent promotional offers;
- better service;
- greater convenience or other factors.

The marketing support programme can be tailored to meet those specific requirements both at a general and a sector level. If the analysis identifies the same trend throughout the network, the supplier can take action at a national level to deal with serious competitive threats.

SUPPORTING MARKET SECTOR ACTIVITIES

In the marketing plan, local outlets were asked to identify the sectors they intended to concentrate on. To develop business in these sectors they will utilise a mixture of advertisements, direct mail, promotions, customer loyalty actions and incentive programmes, and the support material should be customised to the market sector.

Direct mail, for example, can be a powerful weapon in sector marketing whereas advertisements may not be specific enough. Advertisements can help to raise the profile of the local network and make general priced offers, but building an offer that is right for each sector demands a targeted approach. Direct mail, customer incentives, customer loyalty actions, sales incentives and joint pro-motions can all be tailored precisely to the needs of the different marketing sectors.

ENSURING CUSTOMER FOCUS

Customer focus is one of the critical activities that every outlet in a network must achieve. Chapter 9, 'Focusing on the customer', explains in detail how to improve local performance in this area, but the marketing plan provides the opportunity to address individual local requirements. Support can operate at a number of different levels:

- introducing the customer focus programme to distributors that have not yet experienced it;
- marketing customer focus programmes to independent distributors that don't have to participate in the programme;
- providing advice and guidance to local outlets that are trying to implement customer focus;
- providing recognition and award schemes to local outlets that are trying to implement a customer focus programme;
- providing recognition to local outlets that have achieved high standards;
- focusing support on areas where local outlets are having difficulty meeting standards, or where the particular standard is critical to customer satisfaction.

The level of support can be adjusted to the needs of individual outlets. For example, if one of the customer focus standards is laying out the car showroom to meet a certain specification, the support

could take a number of forms depending on the individual circumstances:

- providing detailed building specifications so that the outlet can
  carry out the work itself using its own budgets;
- appointing contractors to handle work throughout the network at
  the manufacturer's expense;
- appointing a project manager to work with local outlets to implement customised solutions;
- providing an advice and guidance service to help local outlets to
  meet the standards themselves.

IMPROVING CUSTOMER SATISFACTION

Customer focus standards should make an important contribution to
achieving high levels of customer satisfaction. However, customer
satisfaction programmes must be adjusted to the standards of individual outlets.

In the marketing plan, the outlets indicated their target customer
satisfaction index for the next year, for example achieve 78 per cent
customer satisfaction. The index describes the overall performance
of the outlet rather than the performance of individual departments,
but the support programmes can be adjusted to match the strengths
and weaknesses of individual departments.

Suppliers can provide support in a number of forms.

- ensuring that all local staff understand the importance of customer
  satisfaction. This is important when an outlet is new to customer
  satisfaction programmes or where an outlet is performing badly;
- providing programmes that help to improve customer satisfaction
  in specific departments. This helps outlets to make targeted
  improvements and enables the supplier to control the emphasis
  within the overall programme;
- operating recognition schemes, that reward achievement or
  improvement in customer satisfaction. If the network as a whole is
  achieving high levels of customer satisfaction the recognition programme should be used to reward excellence with high-value

awards, but if satisfaction levels are poor, then the programme should be adjusted to reflect improvements in standards with a higher number of outlets qualifying for lower-value awards;

- some suppliers have introduced minimum customer satisfaction levels as a qualification for participating in certain programmes or entitlement to rebates. They see customer satisfaction as essential to the future of their business and they are not prepared to leave it to the discretion of individual outlets.

DEVELOPING SKILLS

Chapter 8, 'Achieving consistent standards', provides detailed guidelines on the development of skills and explains the alternatives available. The marketing plan links the development of local skills to the achievement of marketing objectives and focuses attention on the skills needed to succeed in individual sectors. The supplier can support skills development in a number of ways:

- explain the importance of training to local management teams;
- provide a training advisory service to help local outlets identify individual requirements;
- offer a choice of training courses and modules to meet general training needs;
- provide a branch-based training service to handle the training requirements of individual outlets;
- co-operate with training organisations to develop customised training services for local outlets;
- provide a training information or support service to groups that have their own training service.

This is a training support programme that can be tailored easily to individual training requirements. Local outlets can develop individually to meet their own market requirements.

IMPROVING SALESFORCE PERFORMANCE

The marketing plan reinforced the important role of the salesforce and showed that local marketing success can depend on the skills and resources available. Salesforce performance can be supported in a number of ways:

- setting up training programmes to provide personal sales skills and knowledge on selling in specific sectors of the market;
- providing effective product information to ensure that the salesforce has all the information it needs;
- generating enquiries through local and national advertising;
- operating incentive programmes to encourage sales effort;
- co-ordinating sales and marketing actions with local outlets to ensure complete solutions.

While many of these programmes and activities are standard for outlets throughout the network they can be customised to individual needs through the marketing plan and the local skills analysis which identifies how many sales staff are in the branch, what skills they have and how well they are achieving national and local targets.

GENERATING ENQUIRIES

While the local outlet can make strong efforts to improve sales performance at local level, the supplier can provide a consistent input to the sales effort by improving the level of enquiries coming into the branch. This can happen in two ways:

- providing support for local outlets to operate their own pro-grammes to generate enquiries through advertisements, pro-motions, special events or targeted direct mail;
- running major national campaigns to encourage customers and prospects to contact the outlet.

The decision on which way to pitch the support depends on how well established and branded the products are and how effective the local network is.

- If a new product is launched or if the products are not established in the marketplace, it is more important that the supplier runs national advertisements and promotions to raise the profile of the product; the name of the local outlet would be a subsidiary element.

- When the product is established the national and local campaigns can run in parallel with local advertisements pointing out that a particular outlet now stocks certain products.
- Supporting an expanding network puts more emphasis on branding the outlets. 'Product x is now available nationally from a network of authorised distributors and your local stockist is y.'

OFFERING CUSTOMER INCENTIVES

The marketing plan may show that customer incentives are important at national or local level.

- If a supplier is expanding the local network or wants to generate higher levels of showroom traffic across the network, competitions or other incentives can be used to encourage customers into the outlets.
- If the network is performing inconsistently, incentives can be used at local level to improve individual performance.
- If an outlet is receiving a high level of enquiries but not converting them to sales, it may require a different form of customer incentive to overcome poor salesforce performance.

IMPROVING CUSTOMER LOYALTY

Customer loyalty can be influenced by national campaigns that make special offers to customers to increase levels of repeat purchase, but customer loyalty can be influenced indirectly by building individual relations at local level. An analysis of current sales performance by customer will indicate how much repeat business is being handled, compared with national trends. In the case of the car dealer, it operates at two levels.

- Are customers coming back to buy another car after two to three years?

- Are they making use of the dealership's other facilities during the period between major purchases?

Using this analysis the supplier can identify individual actions that can be taken to transform occasional users and prospects into regular customers. Database management is essential here and the manufacturer must ensure that distributors understand the importance of maintaining records on all their customers so that they can set up and maintain individual contact programmes. The more specific the targeting the better, but the company should also support the distributor with loyalty programmes which operate at a general level.

- Is customer loyalty weak in specific sectors such as used-car purchase? Loyalty could be improved with special extended warranties and economy servicing offers to used-car customers.
- Boosting the service business with offers of a discount on the next service or low-priced offers of accessories for customers who take out service contracts.

MAKING THE BEST USE OF ADVERTISING

The next few sectors of this chapter focus on how suppliers can best provide distributors with the deliverables they need to operate their marketing programmes. The assessment of advertising requirements begins with an analysis of the local outlet's current activities:

- Does it have its own budget and does it currently run an advertising campaign?
- How does that advertising campaign meet the supplier's and the local outlet's objectives?
- Is the campaign operating successfully?
- Can it be integrated with the supplier's national campaigns?
- Would the local outlet benefit from additional advertising in terms of higher levels of enquiry or improved awareness and image?
- Would the campaign benefit from greater quality or greater frequency, i.e. does it need professional input and higher budgets?

This initial analysis of the local budget and advertising activities determines how a supplier might integrate its own advertising activities and provide levels of professional support to the local outlet; this could take the form of:

- advice and guidance;
- funds;
- artwork;
- an agency service.

However, if the local outlet has no advertising activity of its own, the supplier has to decide whether the local outlet will benefit from advertising and what form it should take:

- Would an advertising campaign help to raise awareness of the outlet or the supplier in the local market?
- Would it raise the number of enquiries?
- Could the advertising be used to reach the local outlet's selected target market or would direct mail do that more effectively?
- Does the supplier have the budget and the resources to support the individual outlet effectively, or would it be better to support a group of outlets with generic advertising?

The supplier can then decide whether to provide support in the form of:

- financial support for a do-it-yourself operation;
- a kit that provides all the material needed to produce standard advertisements;
- an agency service, which provides advice and guidance plus the facilities to produce and place advertisements for the local outlet.

SUPPORTING DIRECT MARKETING

The requirements for direct marketing are assessed in a similar way to advertising. The local outlet may already be carrying out a direct marketing operation, but may not have the facilities to do it effectively. One of the key questions in the analysis is whether advertising should be used in preference to direct marketing. If the local outlet has good customer records and can identify key sectors where it can make individual offers, direct marketing is likely to produce more effective results.

For example, if the car dealer wanted to expand small fleet sales, the target market would be tightly specified and it should be easy to identify the most important prospects. By analysing progress and response on each of the most important prospects, it is possible to develop a planned direct marketing programme that will move them towards purchase with a series of structured offers.

To achieve this kind of targeted and structured direct marketing, the supplier would have to provide high levels of advice and guidance plus support with developing a database and the provision of professionally-produced mailing pieces. The supplier can either work closely with the local outlet to develop a joint direct-marketing programme or can provide a selection of standard and customised mailing pieces which provides the local outlet with all the support needed.

HELPING LOCAL OUTLETS RUN SPECIAL CAMPAIGNS

A special campaign such as a new product launch is critical to both supplier and local outlet, providing an opportunity for both to benefit from increased public awareness and interest. The supplier must ensure that the effectiveness of the national launch programme for a new product is not weakened by poor performance at local level. The local outlet must be fully briefed on the launch requirements and have the skills and resources to implement the launch programme. In assessing the type of support needed, the supplier has to consider:

- the performance of the local outlet on previous launches;
- the complexity of the launch compared with other launches;
- the level of risk involved in the success or failure of the launch.

This enables the supplier to assess how much support will be provided. The options include:

- appointing a team of representatives to work closely with the local outlet to implement the programme;
- providing a kit or launch guide which includes all the materials needed to launch the product.

RUNNING JOINT PROMOTIONS

Joint promotions between supplier and local outlet can be an effective way of getting further mileage from a marketing budget and boosting the local outlet's performance. In assessing the opportunities and support requirements for joint promotions, the supplier should consider:

- the potential benefit of the joint promotion;
- the level of support required to ensure success;
- the value of the local outlet's contribution;
- the level of involvement the local outlet would have in the operation.

The joint promotion can take the form of advertising, direct mail, promotions and other forms of marketing activity, and these are discussed in detail in other sections of this chapter.

DEVELOPING WHOLESALE ACTIVITIES

The local outlet can develop beyond its own customer base and expand business by operating wholesale activities to support other outlets and retailers that are not competitors. This can also benefit the supplier by ensuring that the business continues to expand beyond the local network without the setting up of a new sales infrastructure. To help the local outlet operate an effective wholesale programme, the supplier has to assess several factors.

- Is the local outlet already operating an effective wholesale programme?
- What is the likely level of business?

- What sort of offers is the local outlet likely to make?
- Has the local outlet got the skills and resources to operate the wholesale programme?
- What form of marketing support will be needed to make the programme work effectively?
- How can the wholesale operation be improved – through stronger sales effort, better incentives, higher-profile advertising or direct mail, use of technology to improve order processing or administration, better stockholding?

OPERATING SALES INCENTIVES

Improving salesforce performance was discussed earlier in the chapter, and an integral part of the process is sales incentives. The supplier can provide support in a number of forms:

- operating an incentive programme for the complete network with national awards for top-performing sales staff. This will help to build general levels of sales performance;
- developing structured sales incentives which cover sales, product knowledge, customer loyalty and many other aspects that improve overall performance;
- developing a programme for individual outlets so that they can improve local performance.

The programme can be customised to individual performance and ensure that local outlets can respond to the needs of individual sales staff.

INTRODUCING NEW TECHNOLOGY

In the marketing plan, new technology was shown to be a means of improving the quality of customer service by reducing the amount of time and effort spent on administration and other non-sales activities. Introducing new technology to a local outlet can take a considerable amount of time and effort if the investment is not to be wasted, and if the outlet is to make full and effective use of the new technology. For example, in introducing a new service database a supplier has to deal with the following issues.

- Who will install the database?
- Who will train local staff on its use?
- Where can staff get advice and guidance on using the database or get help when they have a query?
- Who will monitor the performance of the new technology and decide when modifications have to be made?

INTERNAL RESOURCES

By using the information provided in the marketing plan the supplier can assess the type and level of support needed at each individual outlet; it must also decide whether it has the resources to deliver and manage the programme. Chapter 14, 'Controlling local support programmes', shows how to use internal and external resources to greatest effect to deliver the optimum form of support in a cost-effective way. Once a supplier has analysed the individual marketing plans of all the outlets in the network and integrated those with its own national support programmes, it then has to decide the most efficient method of delivering that service.

RESPONDING TO A LOCAL MARKETING PLAN

This assessment can be used to develop comprehensive support strategies for the entire network or individual programmes based on the marketing plans supplied by each outlet. This is an example of a proposal to an individual outlet.

(1)   OBJECTIVES
We will provide you with a comprehensive support programme so that we can meet our joint objectives of achieving the highest levels of customer satisfaction and building effective long-term customer relationships so that we can ensure future turnover and profitability.

(2)   SWOT
Your area representative will be working with you to establish priorities and action plans that deal with the concerns highlighted in the SWOT analysis. The area representative will agree a timetable for action and will meet you monthly to review progress.

(3)   IDENTIFYING MARKET SECTORS
We will provide you with national data on our performance in each of the key market sectors. Your area representative will work with you to correlate this with data from your territory so that you can assess the most important sectors in your territory. We have appointed a market research company to provide local research support to our dealers. If you want to use their services, ask your area representative to arrange a meeting.

(4)   COMPETITIVE ACTIVITY
We will provide you with national data on competitive activity and offer you the support of a market research company to support your local research activities. We will send you monthly reports on national and regional price trends and provide monthly updates on competitive activity. Your area representative will work with you to monitor local competitive activity and develop suitable responses.

(5)   MARKET SECTOR ACTIVITIES
You have identified your key sector-marketing tasks in the marketing plan. We will be running national advertising programmes to demonstrate our corporate strength in each of the sectors. We will provide you with marketing communications material to support your initiatives and we will provide advice and guidance to help you implement business programmes in each of the sectors. Your area representative will work with your management team to assess priorities and monitor progress. We will also introduce a performance recognition scheme aimed at staff who will contribute to the success of sector programmes.

(6) CUSTOMER FOCUS STANDARDS

We have introduced a set of customer focus standards that are critical to our long-term business success. Your area representative will work with you to assess how well you comply with the standards and discuss an action programme to ensure you meet the standards by the end of the second quarter. These standards are mandatory and we will provide advice and guidance to help you meet them.

(7) CUSTOMER SATISFACTION OBJECTIVES

Your target customer satisfaction index for the coming year is 83, an increase of 5 per cent on the current year. The basis of measuring customer satisfaction will remain the same and you will be issued with responses once a month, with detailed reports on your performance four times a year. To help you improve your customer satisfaction performance, we will be introducing a number of new customer care programmes, and you will be briefed on these at the regional business meetings.

(8) DEVELOPING SKILLS

We have given your dealership skills profile to our training manager and he will contact your training co-ordinator to jointly develop a training programme for the medium and long term. We will continue to offer a full range of training courses from our national training centre and we will be extending the scope of our on-site retail training service.

(9) SALESFORCE PERFORMANCE

We have introduced a new sales representative guild to improve professional standards. Your sales team will be invited to participate in the programme and we will provide them with full details of the incentive schemes, product training programmes and national awards that will be integrated into the guild.

(10) GENERATING ENQUIRIES

You have identified the specific actions your dealership will be taking to generate enquiries. We will provide you with promotional material to support your initiatives and your area representative will work with you to develop your dealership database. We will supplement the information on your dealership database with leads generated through national advertising campaigns.

(11)   CUSTOMER INCENTIVES

Seasonal promotions have played an important role in attracting customers to the showroom or service reception. We will be enhancing the promotional programme to build even higher levels of business and we will be increasing the support budget for individual outlets.

(12)   CUSTOMER LOYALTY

You have identified your key sector marketing activities. It is important that you build the loyalty of existing customers in those sectors, as well as attracting new prospects. Your area representative will work with you to analyse your customer database and identify opportunities for loyalty-building actions. The dealership guide to building customer loyalty outlines the actions you can take.

(13)   ADVERTISING

To ensure that you remain first choice in your territory for sales, parts and service, we will continue to operate the priced-offer advertising programme. The dealer advertising agency will contact you to draw up an advertising schedule for the year. Your target spend should be £xxx over the year and we will continue to offer you a rebate on your costs. Part of your budget should be allocated to generic advertising to increase awareness of the full range of your services and the balance allocated to meeting your sector marketing objectives.

(14)   DIRECT MAIL

Direct mail will help you maintain contact with your customers and will be a valuable tool in developing sector business. The group direct mail agency will provide you with suitable promotional material for each of the sectors and will handle the mailing campaigns on your behalf

(15)   SPECIAL CAMPAIGNS

This year sees the launch of a new executive model which will have a significant impact on fleet and private business. You will be receiving shortly your launch-planning guide, and your area representative will arrange a meeting to review the important launch actions. We will provide a full programme of local and national support for the launch and the material will be available from the end of the first quarter.

(16)   WHOLESALE ACTIVITIES
You have identified parts wholesaling as an important part of your business. We have a range of programmes to support your marketing efforts and we will be negotiating a special discount structure which will enable you to compete more effectively. We have developed a special training programme for wholesale specialists and a member of your staff will be invited to participate.

(17)   SALES INCENTIVE PROGRAMMES
We have changed the emphasis in our incentive programmes to encourage overall professional development rather than short-term sales. The incentive programmes are now incorporated in the sales professional guild described earlier in the proposal and will reward training achievements, product knowledge and repeat-business levels as well as sales volume.

(18)   NEW TECHNOLOGY
We will be introducing the new dealership administration system this year. Your system will be operational by the end of the second quarter and you will shortly receive full details of the implementation and training programme. The new business administration programme based on the system will be launched at regional business meetings, and the group business development team will discuss your specific requirements with your management team.

(19)   REVIEWING THE PROGRAMME
This is our proposal for supporting the development of your dealership business over the next twelve months. Your area representative will review the programmme with you and finalise budgets for the programme.

This proposal provides specific details of the supplier's support proposals for the coming year. The proposal refers to the local outlet's own plans summarised in the marketing plan and indicates that the area representative will be closely involved in putting the proposals into operation. The plan also makes reference to existing publications where these contain relevant information. The proposal is designed to help both parties understand their responsibilities in developing local business.

SUMMARY

This chapter has looked at the support options available to meet a number of different local marketing tasks. This is a first stage in developing a tailored marketing programme that meets the requirements of individual outlets. This chapter shows how information from the local marketing plan can be used to develop a local support strategy. It reviews the support options available against each of the categories in the marketing plan and shows how to select the right option for different situations. It covers the following topics: setting overall objectives, assessing strengths and weaknesses, dealing with competitive activity, supporting market sector activities, ensuring customer focus, improving customer satisfaction, developing skills, improving salesforce performance, generating enquiries, offering customer incentives, improving customer loyalty, making the best use of advertising, supporting direct marketing, helping local outlets to run special campaigns, running joint promotions, developing wholesale activities, operating sales incentives, and introducing new technology. The chapter also describes the internal resources needed to provide different levels of support and provides an example of a supplier's response to a local marketing plan to show how suppliers can present their support programmes to the local outlet.

ACTION CHECKLIST

This chapter does not have a separate action checklist as it covers the same topics as the previous chapter and includes an example of an action programme.

7

TAILORING MARKETING PROGRAMMES

INTRODUCTION

Marketing programmes are used to provide local outlets with the support they need to build business in their own marketplace. The programmes can operate at two levels:

- the programmes run by suppliers on behalf of all their local outlets;
- the programmes that are provided for outlets to run in their own local markets.

An example of the first programme would be an advertisement running in the specialist engineering or business press: 'Use a Brown Engineering-approved distributor for all your components requirements.' The local variation would be 'All-Components engineering distributor – your local Brown Engineering stockist'. Vauxhall's Network Q television commercials have helped to brand every outlet in the network but, at a local level, the outlets would advertise their special offers in the local media. N&P Building Society recently ran a recruitment advertisement for a public relations officer to support the local branches in building community relations in their regions. This community relations programme, developed at local level and co-ordinated by head office staff, was to be fully integrated with the Society's national television and press advertising campaign which built awareness of the N&P brand.

Marketing programmes such as consumer offers or competitions may 'only be available at participating dealerships'. This does not imply that they are customised for local use; it only shows that the programmes are running in limited areas. Price-based promotional programmes – where local outlets are provided with a standard advertisement format into which they can build their own selection of priced offers together with their own branch information – are probably the most widely used local marketing programmes. A further variation of this is the dealer direct-mail service where an agency holds a central database of local addresses and sends customised mail shots to those customers.

Another variation is the promotional kit which provides general guidelines on developing local advertisements and marketing programmes from a series of modular elements. This type of kit contains a guide to planning and operating campaigns plus suggested creative themes and details of any support services available. Some suppliers may have the resources to hire local marketing support staff who provide professional advice and guidance to local outlets.

NATIONAL SUPPORT PROGRAMMES

A national support programme is a visible demonstration that the supplier is helping local outlets to market their services. When a supplier wants to recruit new franchisees or build up a local network, part of the promise is that the supplier will help the local outlet to build business.

Building strong network identity

A national support programme can help to build a strong brand identity for a network of branches and assure customers that they will receive a high standard of service wherever they see the sign. An approach like this is important when the network consists of a fragmented group of independent branches which have no cohesive identity. The national programme helps to build them into a single unit and enables them to benefit from large national advertising campaigns.

Gucci Timepieces, a member of the world-famous Gucci group which produces high-quality leather goods, wanted to build a strong

UK distributor network and to make consumers aware that they could buy Gucci around the country and get first-class service. Its local support programme included a distributor information pack which described the Gucci philosophy, explained the requirements of the Gucci franchise and outlined the support that Gucci would give to the distributor.

To launch the brand, Gucci ran a national advertising campaign in prestige publications and enclosed a reply coupon encouraging prospects to write for the name of their local distributor. The prospects were sent the name of the distributor and were also given a leaflet explaining the standard of service they should expect from the distributor. The distributors were provided with a wide range of merchandising material so that they could brand their own outlets. As part of the continuing programme of national support, Gucci ran major national advertising campaigns during the peak gift-buying seasons when sales were at their highest levels. Gucci's national campaigns were raising awareness of its national network and helping to build its business.

During the running boom of the 1980s, the major sports shoe manufacturers such as Nike, Puma, Adidas, Reebok and New Balance sought to increase their share of the market by building retailer loyalty. Although most sports retailers carried multiple brands, there were a number of attempts to create single brand superstores such as the Adidas Connection – where staff were specially trained in the product and the store provided equipment and products not available in other stores. Without that kind of formal branding the shoe manufacturers could not achieve high levels of recognition for their retail outlets. Sports retailing has experienced branding at a more general level with the emergence of multiple retailers such as Olympus and Champion Sports that can provide their local branches with the depth of national advertising and a strong brand identity that is not available to the independents.

Other suppliers have tried to build the reputation of their local outlets with a phrase like, 'the sign of a good . . .' which explains the benefits of dealing with a particular retail outlet. Advertising is used as part of a long-term strategic marketing programme to build awareness and confidence in the local network, but a national support campaign contains more than just advertising.

Strategic promotion

National promotional campaigns are used to attract customers for short or long periods. Esso Tiger Tokens, a programme that has now become the Esso Collection is both tactical and strategic. Its tactical value is that it can encourage customers to switch between brands to obtain free gifts and it takes the emphasis away from price difference. But in the long term it is a valuable strategic branding programme. The Esso Collection includes a choice of quality merchandise presented in a well-produced 'lifestyle' catalogue, and the high product values encourage brand loyalty by ensuring that customers keep buying Esso petrol to achieve their gifts. A national promotional campaign like this is fully integrated with the national advertising campaign which stresses the quality of the petrol and the broad range of products and services available from an Esso outlet.

Imposing corporate identity

As well as promotions, national support programmes can also include the development of corporate identities to ensure that customers recognise the qualities and brand values of the outlet. This can take a very simple form where a supplier provides stickers, signs or other visual material that indicates that this is a ** outlet. On the premises of an outlet that handles a wide range of products and services from different suppliers the results can be visually disastrous, but franchised outlets can usually be controlled more effectively, provided they are given clear guidelines on how to use the material that is supplied. Chapter 8, 'Achieving consistent standards', covers the subject of corporate identity in more detail.

The introduction of a new corporate identity is an opportunity to promote the values and benefits of dealing with the network. When Case Europe, the construction and agricultural equipment manufacturer, introduced a new identity for its distributors throughout Europe, it ran a series of ads in the trade press to explain the reasons for the change and the quality of service that stood behind the new identity.

MANDATORY PROGRAMMES

While national support programmes have benefits for both supplier and local outlet, there are a number of programmes that are crucial to achieving the right standards of customer service. These programmes give the supplier a degree of control over critical local operations. Chapter 9, 'Focus on customer care', explains the benefits of focusing the attention of branch staff on customer satisfaction.

When Ford introduces customer satisfaction programmes such as Courtesy Car, it is essential that every dealership participates because the programmes are designed to increase service business by improving customer convenience. Although the dealers have discretion in the way they operate the programme at local level, it is vital that every dealership offers the service because it is an integral part of the customer care programme.

Martin the Newsagent ran a promotion to build store traffic and demonstrate that it offered real value for money. The promotion, which offered customers who purchased a certain range of products in Martin stores the opportunity to take part in a prize draw, depended on full participation by all outlets to ensure that the promotion was acceptable to all the manufacturers and could be publicised on a national level. Part of the offer was that customers could find a Martin's outlet within easy reach wherever they were in the country.

Training programmes that improve the quality of customer service are an integral part of a local marketing support programme. Although the courses and the method of delivery can be tailored to suit local markets and the local skills profile, participation must be mandatory to ensure that all branches deliver a consistently high standard of service. Programmes that are mandatory should be built into the local franchise agreement.

PARTICIPATION IN OTHER PROGRAMMES

Not all support programmes are mandatory. By offering local outlets a choice of programmes, suppliers can tailor their marketing to suit local market conditions. The other programmes might include:

- local advertising;
- direct mail;
- product literature;
- display material;
- merchandising material;
- competitions;
- special offers;
- public relations support;
- community activities.

These are programmes that can be used tactically to build sales, but they do not influence the long-term strategic branding that is important to the development of the network. Suppliers can produce a guide to support programmes, which enables the local outlets to select programmes that allow them to develop their own promotional strategies. The guides should:

- explain the scope and benefits of individual programmes;
- describe the support material available to operate the programme;
- explain how to order support material;
- provide guidelines on running the programmes.

Many suppliers have tried to avoid serious levels of support by providing an ad-hoc collection of support material. This is not the same as providing business support and it should not be used as a substitute for serious planning.

TAILORING PROGRAMMES

The value of mandatory national support campaigns is that they minimise the cost of support management by providing standard programmes with the minimum of extra effort. However, the programmes may offer limited benefit and may build the long-term branding without being responsive to short-term sales requirements. Market support programmes must have the flexibility to be easily customised without sacrificing the benefits of volume production.

MODULAR SUPPORT PROGRAMMES

The Ford 'Selling Service' programme was designed as a modular kit which could be tailored easily to local conditions. The kit was in the form of an 'action pack' which contained all the material dealers needed to operate a wide range of business and promotional programmes. To ensure that the programme operated effectively, the field salesforce worked with dealers to analyse the local market and select the programmes that were most appropriate. The dealers also had access to an agency service that provided them with professional support for research, advertising planning and direct marketing as well as supplying a range of customised advertisements and direct mail shots. The support programme was also integrated with a local training initiative which improved the skills of distributor staff. All the ingredients were there to provide a fully-integrated business development programme.

Tailoring the programme through research

The programme was developed to help dealers regain the service business they were losing to independents and chains such as Halfords. Research carried out before the programme was launched identified customers' key concerns over the service they received from franchised dealers and analysed the reasons they preferred other forms of service. This research provided a basis for developing a series of dealership standards and a range of service offers that were right for the market. Dealers were also encouraged to carry out research in their own territories to identify the local competition and their own potential customer base. Priced offers were an essential element of the dealer offer and a research agency was commissioned to carry out nationwide price surveys on a wide range of products and service offers and to work with distributors to develop local pricing strategies.

Mandatory and optional modules

Part of the programme was mandatory to ensure that dealers were able to provide the right standards of service, while the other modules allowed them to attack different sectors of the market. The mandatory modules were based on a series of customer focus standards and the dealers were given guidelines on how to achieve them.

A range of other modules provided dealers with plans, programmes and support material to develop effective marketing strategies for different market sectors. For example, it covered selling service to business users, women, the used-car market and high-profile motorists. It also provided detailed plans for setting up customer events such as a women's workshop or for establishing a 'quickfit' type operation for selling fast-moving exhausts, tyres or batteries in competition with independent specialists. Finally, the guide included a series of priced-offer advertisements and seasonal promotions which could be customised with the dealer's name, address and price-offers.

To put the programme into operation, dealers were asked to prepare a business plan and marketing strategy, together with an allocation of budget based on current and forecast turnover. Ford would then agree its contribution to the programme and the dealer launched the programme.

Business development options

A similar modular approach was taken by the German car paint manufacturer, Spies Hecker, which sold a wide range of products to franchised and independent bodyshops. Although distributors had received extensive marketing support in the past, it was apparent that marketing support alone would not be sufficient to help the bodyshops improve their performance. The bodyshop was an important part of the entire car dealership operation and made a significant and growing contribution to overall turnover and profit. With the increasing levels of competition and the higher levels of investment needed to provide a quality service, it was important that the bodyshop ran an efficient business operation. Spies Hecker worked closely with the local distributor to provide the right level of support to the bodyshop.

The support programme was based on a programme called 'Partners in Profit', which incorporated a wide range of support materials used to put a bodyshop business plan into operation.

- The first part of the programme is a bodyshop self-analysis, which enables the bodyshop manager to analyse the current business and future prospects in a logical way and formulate plans based on that. The guide leads the bodyshop manager through a series of questions relating to:
  - the type of customers;
  - prospects;
  - competition;
  - business conditions.
  The bodyshop can then build up a clear picture of its customer base and competitive activity.

- The next stage is to analyse strengths and weaknesses as a basis for building a bodyshop action plan. The strengths and weaknesses section asks bodyshops questions about the way they handle different aspects of their business. The analysis also provides information that can be used to build up copy for advertisements and direct mail.
- When the bodyshop staff have completed their self-analysis, they put together a business plan which is reviewed in conjunction with the local distributor and the Spies Hecker sales representative. The business plan incorporates the actions they will take together with their advertising and marketing proposals.

Spies Hecker is then in a position to provide help at a number of levels. The 'Partners in Profit' programme incorporates a number of different modules to improve the business and an increasing number are supplied on software for use on personal computers. By providing management and accounting packages, Spies Hecker can ensure that the bodyshop improves its financial performance and control, throughput, productivity and workshop loading.

Financial performance depends on good control and the business packages ensure that bodyshops understand every aspect of their financial performance and provide a competitively-priced and pro-fitable service to customers. The 'Partners in Profit' programme also includes technical advisory and planning services to ensure that bodyshops are able to take advantage of the latest refinishing tech-niques.

The value of this programme to Spies Hecker is that it encourages and supports a programme of self development. Distributors are able to take advantage of the modular package and work closely with their customers to tailor the programme to their requirements. The elements of the programme are planned and produced centrally, but the programme operates independently at local level.

DIRECT MARKETING

The essence of an effective local support programme is that local outlets understand their customers' needs and provide a level of service that is tailored to that market. In terms of customer satisfac-tion, the most powerful weapon available to companies is direct marketing.

Targeting individual customers

Direct marketing is a form of communications in which individual messages are sent to individual customers. Direct-mail letters are the best-known form of direct marketing and a simple example illustrates the difference between advertising, which aims to reach the widest possible audience at the lowest cost per contact, and direct mail which aims at one-to-one contact.

A lawn mower manufacturer runs a national advertising campaign to attract professional users.

*'The Greengrow Mower is the mower for the professional user; it
produces a superb finish quickly and easily, and is guaranteed for
long reliable operation.'*

This advertisement communicates the key benefits to the professional groundsman, but this direct-mail letter is targeted precisely at
an individual user.

As the head groundsman of County Park, you will be aware of the
pressure that Any Town Corporation is putting on all departments to
reduce their operating costs. The new Greengrow Mower has been
proved in tests to cut a cricket pitch 15 per cent faster than any
competitive mower and still produce a superb finish. You not only reduce
your labour costs, but because we have also increased the service interval
your maintenance costs are lower. We are willing to offer you a 5 per cent
discount on the purchase price because you are a loyal customer and we
will offer you a guaranteed part-exchange price for your old models. Bob
Smith, your local distributor, will be contacting you next week to discuss
terms, but if you would like a demonstration in the meantime, please
contact our national enquiry centre and they will arrange for a visit within
forty-eight hours.

This gets across the same benefits, but it is precisely targeted at an
individual and it makes a very specific offer.

The key to the success of that programme is an understanding of
the local customer and the right level of information on that customer's needs. The database management needed to achieve that
kind of targeting is described in more detail later in this chapter.
Direct marketing can be a powerful weapon in the hands of local
outlets because it enables them to talk to their customers on their own
terms.

Customising local communications

When ICL introduced the Customer Reception Centre, a single point
of contact for customers throughout the country, it realised that
branches would be reluctant to lose day-to-day contact with their
local customers, so it balanced this with a programme of regular

customer care visits which enabled the branch to take a proactive role in communications with customers.

The first stage in the process was a direct mail shot which included a brochure on the benefits of the new central Customer Reception Centre, together with a personalised letter from the local branch manager explaining the changing and more positive role of the branch. The brochure itself was customised with a map showing the location of the branch, and the letter was addressed to customers individually. A mailing like this had the benefit of centralised design and production to ensure quality and consistency, but it bore the name of the local outlet to ensure the right level of contact.

A more conventional use of direct marketing is the specific offer to customers of a local outlet. The Spring Motoring Check is one of a range of seasonal offers made by car dealers to build local service business. Customers are offered a free safety check, plus a report on any service or maintenance needed, together with an estimate. Each dealership nominates its own prices or offers within overall guidelines and is able to make a special seasonal gift offer as an added incentive. The mail shots are produced centrally and overprinted with the detailed local information before central distribution to produce a tailored local offer.

The British Airways Speedwing Training programme, which is described in earlier chapters, relies on carefully targeted direct mail to provide each of the local travel agents in the network with a customised training programme. The training agency develops a database with all the information on local skills and business requirements, and then mails details of individual training programmes to each travel agent. The travel agent receives only relevant information and does not have to sift through unwanted information.

Supporting sector marketing

Although that programme is designed to improve relationships between a company and its agents, the same technique can be used to support travel agents marketing to their customers. Galileo, a company owned by a group of international airlines, provides computerised information and reservation systems to travel agents. Using the

Galileo system, a travel agent can offer customers a fast efficient service that is vital to winning and retaining business. To help travel agents communicate the benefits to their customers, Galileo developed a series of direct-mail programmes aimed at different sectors of the market such as business travellers, package-holiday customers and special-interest holidays. A series of letters and offers is available to the travel agents for customisation on their own personal computer systems and the letters have identified variables for modification by the travel agent.

The programme can be modified easily to suit the individual travel agent's own customer profile. If, for example, the agent handles a high level of business travel and the agent has information on the travelling patterns of its customers, it could offer special deals on car hire, hotels and entertainment for the travellers' regular destinations. It could also ensure that individual business travellers took full advantage of the 'frequent flyer' offers made by many of its major airlines.

Air UK, an independent airline based at Stansted, provided its travel agents with a customised mailing service based on knowledge of business-travel destinations. It had identified, through analysis of customer patterns, that a high level of business was coming from companies in financial engineering and the oil business using regional airports to fly staff to and from London via Stansted. The company ran a series of advertisements in local newspapers within the catchment areas of the regional airports to build the perception of Air UK and Stansted as the most efficient way to meet domestic and regional travel needs and then worked in conjunction with local travel agents to develop a direct-marketing programme aimed at the most important market sectors.

The travel agents identified the companies within their regions that fitted the travelling profile – head office or branch in the region and other branches or head office in London or one of the regional airports. They mailed these companies with introductory information on the Air UK service and offered to carry out an analysis of their UK travel requirements. The agent then operated a regular mailing programme, which included special offers for regular travellers together with personalised gifts. This direct marketing was integrated with the national and regional advertising campaign and demonstrates the value of co-operation between an operator and agents.

DATABASE MANAGEMENT

The key to the success of all these programmes is detailed knowledge of the local customer base so that the offers and information can be tailored to local marketing programmes. The most efficient way to handle this is to maintain a central database of all local customers and use database-management techniques to manage the mailing list. Local outlets are unlikely to have the sophisticated equipment needed to carry out database-management operations and the exercise can be carried out more efficiently on a central database.

Contents of the database

The database would contain the names and addresses of each outlet's customers, together with variable information such as:

- purchasing patterns;
- size of expenditure;
- type of purchase;
- number of employees;
- other variations depending on the type of business.

Some examples illustrate how the database can be utilised to produce targeted mailing lists. The title describes the product and the list represents different members of the target audience.

TRAVEL AGENCY TRAINING SERVICES

- all travel agencies;
- agencies belonging to a multiple group;
- independent agencies;
- agencies with a turnover in excess of . . .;
- agencies with less than . . . staff;
- sales staff responsible for business travel;
- sales staff responsible for holiday travel;

- middle managers with budget responsibility for training;
- staff with less than one year's travel agency experience;
- staff with specific qualifications.

TRAVEL AGENCY CUSTOMERS

- business travellers;
- leisure travellers;
- special-interest leisure travellers;
- long-haul travellers;
- domestic/European business travellers;
- frequent flyers who cover more than . . . miles per year;
- first class leisure travellers.

CAR DEALERSHIP

- private owners;
- business users;
- fleet operators;
- fleet operators with more than . . . vehicles;
- new-car buyers in their third year of ownership;
- used-car buyers;
- older drivers;
- service customers;
- bodyshop customers.

The database can be broken down into categories that correspond to market sectors and the categories can become increasingly specific.

Building the database

Information for the database can be gathered from a number of sources, including:

- local customer sales records;
- replies to advertisements;
- responses to special offers or invitations;
- applications for membership;
- market research.

The initial database is unlikely to be complete or provide information in the most suitable format, so companies that wish to benefit from direct-marketing run special campaigns to gather appropriate information. For example, an invitation to an open evening or a prize draw would require customers to provide information that is essential for the database.

Local outlets can be given guidelines on the way to build and maintain their own records so that they provide suitable input to the database. The database is then built (the techniques of database management are beyond the scope of this book) and a series of mailings run to meet business and marketing objectives. By managing the process centrally and working in close conjunction with local outlets, suppliers can ensure that their local outlets enjoy a professional-quality direct-marketing service that is precisely tailored to their local market.

LOCAL EVENT MANAGEMENT

Local events such as open evenings, trade shows and customer receptions are a powerful method of building customer loyalty, but they need to be handled professionally to achieve the right results. By providing the right level of support, suppliers can help local outlets develop a programme of events that is appropriate for their local market. The support includes:

- the development of suitable promotional and display material;
- the theme for the event;
- the invitations and generation of mailing lists;
- support literature;
- personal support by members of the head-office team.

When Pitman launched the Institute of Management book series, it was described as the UK's biggest business book launch. A central feature of the launch was a series of customer events run in conjunction with regional bookshops around the country. The bookshops were given detailed guidelines on the programme and provided with mailing letters inviting customers to the launch event.

The bookshops put together their own mailing lists utilising account information, local education establishments and membership information from the local branch of the Institute of Management.

At the event, one of the authors attended to make a brief presentation and talk to customers, and a group of Pitman sales and editorial staff joined with bookshop staff to host the evening and meet customers. Pitman also provided window displays and free-standing display units to ensure a consistent event standard. By providing a professional support service, Pitman was able to ensure a consistent standard and give the bookshops the freedom to develop an event that was right for the local market.

Other suppliers provide the services of professional event organisers to help local outlets organise more complex customer events. An incentive scheme for a high-street bank offered business customers a structured series of special sporting prizes. Customers were awarded points for using different types of business banking services and could win a day's free participation and coaching in different types of sporting event such as gliding, water sports, outward bound, motor racing and other activities that had high levels of appeal to the target audience.

The local branches could tailor the awards to their own customer base, but they did not have to provide the resources to manage the events themselves; this was handled by a specialist organisation which could set up the events in different parts of the country.

CUSTOMISED ADVERTISING SERVICE

Local or regional advertising campaigns can be customised to suit the needs of the local market. Support can be delivered in a number of forms:

- funds to enable local outlets to produce and run their own advertisements;
- contributions to the cost of joint supplier/local outlet advertisements;
- contributions to the cost of advertisements run by regional groups of outlets;

- production of national support advertisements that incorporate local information and which are run on a regional basis;
- support for advertisements run in conjunction with regional radio or television stations.

Funding options

The level of support depends on the funds available for local support and the outlet's own budget. For example, many independent outlets have substantial advertising budgets of their own and utilise the suppliers' budgets to supplement their own or to run specific campaigns. Other smaller outlets or franchised outlets without their own budgets rely entirely on the supplier's contribution to run local campaigns. Because of this, the question of financial support is usually subject to negotiation.

Supplying advertising material

The more practical forms of support – complete advertisements, logos, artwork, photographs – can be supplied for inclusion in the outlet's own local campaigns. The supplier is likely to be more concerned about the consistency of local advertisements than the local outlet, and should issue clear guidelines on the use of different elements of corporate identity. Many suppliers provide advertising standard manuals which give examples of layouts for different sizes of advertisements, explain the position and size of the company name and logo, list the typefaces to use and include sample advertisements for guidance.

Centralised advertising services

Alternatively, the supplier can offer local outlets a central advertising service. This support policy enables suppliers to offer local outlets consistent professional advertisement standards, with local information such as name and address, map, priced offers, product variations and special offers incorporated. The local outlet benefits from national advertising and strong branding, but it has advertisements that suit the local market as well.

Advertising in test markets

Local advertising support can also be used in test markets. Here, the company can vary price, product or promotional support to evaluate the effect of different programmes. In consumer-goods marketing, many suppliers utilise the marketing services offered by regional television, press or radio. The media provide the demographic and market information on their region and the suppliers can then develop a suitable local campaign. The media will also provide support in the form of merchandising and contract research into the needs of the local market. The supplier places advertisements in the media and is able to evaluate the effectiveness of the campaign.

Regional advertising programmes

The regional approach can also be used to establish a co-operative advertising programme between groups of local outlets – Southern Vauxhall dealers, Northern Electricity showrooms. Local outlets pool their budgets and are able to build a higher profile by running larger advertisements or advertising more frequently. Each outlet includes its own name and address, but the advertisement promotes the generic benefits of the group.

Some regional advertisements feature priced offers that are available at all the outlets in the group. This requires a high degree of co-operation between local outlets to set the target prices, but suppliers should be aware that the Office of Fair Trading (OFT) may regard this as a form of cartel and suppliers should seek guidance on the procedure for obtaining OFT approval for joint, priced advertisements.

Providing a central form of support for local advertisements not only ensures consistency and good branding, it can also help to make the most of effective use of scarce budgets. By purchasing all advertising space or time centrally, the supplier can negotiate more effective rates based on volume purchase, and can handle all the administration associated with media planning.

SUMMARY

This chapter takes the support process a stage further by reviewing some of the techniques for tailoring support programmes to local market conditions. It shows that national support programmes are important in certain circumstances – building network identity, operating strategic promotions, achieving customer satisfaction or imposing corporate identity. As a result, some support programmes must be mandatory. However, local outlets have the flexibility to participate in other programmes, depending on their business objectives. Modular support programmes are a versatile method of meeting the requirements of different markets, while techniques such as direct marketing enable a local outlet to target individual customers. The chapter explains a number of methods for customising local communications and supporting the sector marketing activities identified in the local marketing plan. Local event management can also be used to allow local outlets to put on events for their customers with the backing of professional organisation. The chapter also looks at methods of customising local advertising, outlining funding options and providing guidelines for advertising in test markets and developing regional advertising programmes.

ACTION CHECKLIST

MANDATORY PROGRAMMES

How important are national support programmes to the development of your network?

Do you need to build a strong network identity or impose consistent visual standards across national or international networks?

Are you planning strategic promotions that are crucial to your long-term success?

Are there programmes that are integral to achieving high levels of customer satisfaction?

Do you need to ensure that each outlet possesses certain customer care skills?

Do you have the degree of control to impose these programmes on the network?

PARTICIPATION

Can you identify programmes that are important, but not essential to the success of your network?

Are the programmes sufficiently easy to run to be used by local outlets?

Can the programmes be adapted easily to local market conditions?

Can you present tactical programmes in a modular form so that they can be adapted easily for local use?

Would a modular approach allow you to meet different market requirements without fragmenting the strength of your identity?

Can you back the modular approach with a professional support service to ensure that local outlets make effective use of the modules?

Can the modular programmes be adapted easily to international use?

DIRECT MARKETING

Is advertising or direct marketing more appropriate for reaching your local customers?

Are local markets well segmented?

Do you and your outlets have sufficient information on customers to operate targeted direct marketing programmes?

Do you have a customer database and do local outlets contribute to it?

Would national legislation impact on your direct marketing programmes?

Can you customise your local communications material to provide local outlets with a more personal service?

Do you have central facilities for customising direct marketing material for local branches?

Does the customised material retain a strong corporate identity?

Do you have the resources to manage large-scale database marketing operations across an international network?

EVENT MANAGEMENT

Are customer events important to building effective relationships with local customers?

Can you manage these events professionally, using central resources?

If not, do you provide your local outlets with clear guidelines on event management?

ADVERTISING SUPPORT

Is local advertising important to your local marketing objectives?

What is the scale of your local advertising programme?

Can the advertisements be standardised or do they vary from market to market?

Would international advertising campaigns be appropriate to your networks?

Do customised local advertisements retain a strong sense of corporate identity?

Do your international teams work with their own local advertising agencies?

Do your local outlets develop their own advertisements?

How can you ensure that they contribute to your objectives?

8

ACHIEVING CONSISTENT STANDARDS

INTRODUCTION

'The problem is that each of the outlets perform at a different level. I want every customer who buys from one of our branches to know immediately that they are in a . . .'

The quotation underlines the problems that companies marketing through multiple outlets face – how to provide customers with consistent standards of service. Many commentators argue that it doesn't matter because customers are unlikely to visit more than one outlet so they will not be making comparisons. The key issue is how to attract prospects to an outlet in the first place and turn them into customers.

Advertising that says 'you'll find more choice at our supermarket or enjoy better service at our fast-food outlet' is delivering a promise that every outlet bearing the name will offer a certain level of quality. If the outlet does not deliver that promise the customer will be disappointed and will not return. There are also certain types of retail outlet where customers are likely to visit a number of different locations – hotels, petrol stations, banks, restaurant chains and airlines. Customers *do* have a choice when they are on the move and they will use their experience of the local outlet to judge other locations. While companies may not be able to achieve consistency in every aspect – size of outlet, number of staff, stock levels – these may not be crucial factors. What they must try to control are the factors that influence customer satisfaction – the quality of customer service.

A London resident, on holiday, using a small village bank branch would not expect the same number of service points, the same range of products and services, or even the same opening hours as their main branch, but they would have certain expectations about the type and quality of service they were given.

BRANDING LOCAL OUTLETS

This ability to reproduce consistent standards in every outlet is integral to branding. Customers know what to expect from a Holiday Inn, a Pizza Hut, a BP service station, Habitat store, Martin the Newsagent or Boots the Chemist: each of these outlets has a set of brand values built up over a long period of time in the same way as branded products such as Kellogg's, Cadbury, BMW, Marks and Spencer, P&O, Black & Decker. Customers immediately assume that the product must be good because a brand leader would not market a poor product.

Using branding to grow a new network

By applying the same approach to retail outlets and branches, companies hope to achieve the same levels of customer awareness. During the 1980s, financial institutions used the branding approach to build up networks of estate agents to take full advantage of the current property boom. Small regional networks and independent agents became branches of such organisations as Prudential Properties, Black Horse Agencies and many others. The people and the offices were the same, but the branches now had the backing and support of a major company with access to a nationwide information network and the benefits of integrated management practices. The fact that the housing market collapsed at the end of the 1980s led many companies to withdraw from this type of operation but that should not reflect on its potential long-term benefits.

The same process is in operation in the optician trade where Boots has taken over a network of independent local practices to set up a nationwide chain of Boots Opticians. There were already optician departments within the store, in some larger Boots outlets, but in smaller towns separate outlets have been used to build up the national network. Once again the people and the outlets are the same, but customers now have greater choice, better prices in some cases, and confidence in a brand name. Boots supports the outlet with the backing of advertising, management systems and training. The independent outlets benefit from the higher profile, the Boots brand name and the value of Boots national advertising campaigns to attract higher levels of business.

Branding franchised services

Dairy Crest, the milk distributor, has recently changed the basis of its milk delivery system to try to improve the quality of its service and improve its own-brand performance. It had previously employed its own roundsmen and managed the business directly. It switched in 1992 to a new basis – franchised roundsmen – where each roundsman was responsible for building his own business. Dairy Crest provided business support, training and the vehicle together with administrative support and a selection of promotions and campaigns in which the roundsman could participate. The roundsman was responsible for efficient delivery and collection and could boost his own turnover and profit by selling more milk or selling additional products.

By switching to a franchise agreement, Dairy Crest immediately acquired a committed workforce which should, in theory, boost the group's overall turnover and profit. It also retained an efficient local delivery service at a time when there was an apparent decline in the availability of doorstep services in the wake of increased sales through supermarkets and other convenience outlets. The Dairy Council had already been running a series of television commercials reinforcing the benefits of doorstep delivery. Dairy Crest was able to introduce customer service standards as part of the franchise agreement so that it could also control the quality and consistency of the service.

Consistency and quality of service are crucial to the long-term branding of retail outlets and the key to their achievement is quality standards and the availability of training to achieve those standards.

QUALITY STANDARDS

Chapter 9, 'Focusing on customer care', outlines the key requirements to deliver a quality service to customers. The requirements are qualitative rather than quantitive but these can be translated into measurable targets which local outlets must achieve. This extract from a customer focus manual shows how the process works.

'Branches must conform with our customer focus standards and should achieve the following targets:

- train ** staff from the following departments to achieve quality standards;
- maintain adequate stock cover for £** volume turnover;
- maintain a fleet of delivery vehicles to reach ** customers;
- provide ** square metres of selling space with adequate trained staff to serve ** customers per hour at peak hours;
- respond to written enquiries within ** days;
- keep queue waiting times to ** minutes;
- respond to telephone enquiries within ** minutes;
- aim at delivery within ** hours of order;
- deal with customer queries within ** hours;
- escalate any serious queries that cannot be resolved within ** hours;
- make customer-care visits to top ten customers at least once a month;
- visit all customers within a three-month period.'

This is a very general outline of quality standards that can be applied and adapted to different types of business. Quality standards must be measurable; they should be carefully controlled and, ideally, they should conform to the standards of an independent organisation such as the British Standards Institute (BSI). BSI manages a broad range of standards for products and services. Product standards, for example, mean that products have been manufactured and inspected to extremely tight specifications and customers can feel confident that any batch of products coming from one company or from a number of sources will be consistent.

Quality of local service

The same techniques are now being applied to the quality of service available from a company and BS 5750 is the recognised means of demonstrating that a business conforms to international quality standards in the way it deals with customers. BS 5750 is not a set of rigid standards applied in the same way to every business; the business is measured in a number of different fields that are crucial to the quality of customer service. So BS 5750 would be applied in a different way to a manufacturing company and to a professional services consultancy. Each company is measured and can be compared easily and realistically.

Local performance can therefore be included in the scope of BS 5750. A group of solicitors, for example, who operated a network of local branches decided that it would be worth registering under BS 5750 to demonstrate that they were capable of delivering a quality professional service. The initial assessment was used to identify the critical activities that determined the successful operation of the practice. The assessment covered general activities such as speed of response to telephone and written enquiries, and more specific activities such as time spent in handling conveyancing or searches. Consultants worked with the practice management team to define a unique set of standards and to identify the actions that would be needed to achieve that standard in each of the branches.

The consultants drew up a timetable for achieving the standards and, when the practice had achieved them, it was awarded BS 5750. The process did not stop there because each branch had to continue to meet the performance standards to retain its status as a BS 5750 supplier. The practice was able to control the performance of each of its branches and was able to offer its clients a measurable standard of service.

Measuring customer service

BS 5750 is also at the heart of ICL's Customer Response Strategy which provides a central point of contact for customer enquiries throughout the country. Customer response was previously handled by individual branches dealing with their local customers, but branches did not necessarily have the skills or resources needed to deal with the full range of enquiries. The Customer Response

Strategy is based on a Customer Reception Centre which is accessible twenty-four hours a day at local rates and provides a control centre for providing the customer with the right response. The Customer Reception Centre can draw on various ICL centres of excellence and co-ordinate their activities, keeping the customer fully informed on all aspects of the service.

The Customer Reception Centre, which appears to the customer to be a local branch response, conforms to BS 5750 and provides customers with a quality response to all their queries. Customer reception staff are measured on how quickly they reply to the original call, how quickly they provide a response within specific guidelines and how frequently they keep the customer informed until the task is completed. There is also an integral escalation procedure so that any queries that cannot be handled within target times are immediately handed on to other people within the organisation who have the authority to commit additional resources to the problem. ICL has solved the problem of consistent branch service by handling enquiries centrally, but the programme frees branch staff to carry out more proactive customer care work.

Consistent local quality

BS 5750 is also finding its way into the local service station; a number of Volvo and BMW dealerships, for example, now have service departments that conform to BS 5750 and this provides service customers with a reassurance of quality. Service technicians have always followed the guidelines of manufacturer's approved service schedules, but the new requirements of BS 5750 have added additional inspection processes and different work practices which improve the quality of the service department. For example, incomplete jobs which might be waiting for replacement parts are labelled 'process incomplete' so that the vehicle is not moved accidentally while it is in a possibly dangerous condition. Other aspects of BS 5750 relate to the time taken to complete jobs, presentation and explanation of invoices and procedures for dealing with customer complaints. This improved quality of service and the seal of approval of an independent organisation has helped to enhance the reputation of an area of the motor trade that has traditionally suffered from a poor reputation and it also enables the manufacturer to offer customers a consistent standard of service throughout the branch network.

Measuring customers' expectations of quality

BSI registration provides an independent method of assessing and maintaining the quality of branch performance. Quality can also be assessed in line with customers' expectations of the service. Research into customers' attitudes shows how customers feel about the service that is being delivered. For example, many service organisations provide a questionnaire to customers at the end of every service asking how they rated different aspects of the service. The service engineers are also asked to complete a visit report describing the nature of the problem, the actions they took and the time taken to complete different aspects of the job. By analysing this information and comparing the performance of individual branches and individual engineers, the company can build up a profile of service performance and can take appropriate action to deal with any of the problems.

The performance survey covers such aspects as:

- time to reach customer;
- promptness of arrival;
- time to diagnose;
- availability of replacement parts;
- time to complete the task;
- satisfaction with the standard of work;
- helpfulness of the service engineer.

The fact that part of the measurement is based on actual customer assessment rather than a set of arbitrary standards provides greater credibility to the results and enables them to be presented as part of a customer focus programme. The customer surveys also provide an opportunity to maintain pro-active communication with customers by showing that local outlets respond to customer queries and concerns. Chapter 11, 'Developing a contact strategy', explains this process in more detail.

Measuring performance in quality is, however, only the starting point for achieving consistency. The customer surveys and the quality assessment indicate the key factors to be measured and the level of current achievement. The challenge to the supplier is how to raise and maintain the quality of performance throughout the local network.

SKILLS PROFILE

Performance reviews and customer surveys provide the starting point for developing the skills needed to deliver the highest standard of quality and customer service at each outlet. Performance improvement programmes can be ad-hoc activities designed to improve performance in specific areas or they can be incorporated into branch business development programmes which are designed to improve overall business performance.

The marketing plan, outlined in Chapter 5, should incorporate a skills profile for all the staff who will be involved in meeting the local outlet's business objectives and this provides a basis for planning local training requirements. The profile should be developed by the local manager working in conjunction with a training specialist from the head-office team or from an independent training organisation. The skills profile will detail the number of people required to deliver the various services at branch level and identify the skills they need to provide an efficient professional service. The profile should also assess the experience of key people within the outlet to identify promotion prospects and evaluate the level of management and supervisory skills available.

This skills profile ensures that the training programme can be tailored to the needs of different outlets and of individuals within the outlets. A tailored training programme is more likely to provide the outlet with the right skills to meet its business objectives than an all-purpose training programme that does not recognise differences between local markets. The skills profile and the training plan that is based on it can be used as the basis for a training management database which will ensure that each outlet receives the right training services and the right training information.

The Speedwing Training survey has already been mentioned in earlier chapters. Speedwing Training is the training division of British Airways, originally established to carry out the massive training exercise that British Airways undertook to build its customer service skills before privatisation. The division now uses its customer service training skills and its specialist travel industry knowledge to deliver standard and customised training to companies in the travel business as well as other companies that depend on high standards of customer service. Travel agents represent a high proportion of Speedwing's customer base and, to help agents improve their local marketing performance, Speedwing developed a training partnership programme.

It prepared a questionnaire to help the travel agents identify the skills within their own organisation. Each type of job was assessed, from director or general manager, through to supervisors, sales staff, customer representatives and business or package-holiday specialists. Each member of staff detailed their experience and their qualifications to date. The agency also provided a profile of its business – whether it concentrated on business or holiday travel, or whether it offered specialist services in any particular area.

The profile, together with information on numbers of staff and turnover of the agency, enabled Speedwing to build a training/skills profile which was used to develop individual training roadmaps. The agency appointed a training co-ordinator who was responsible for gathering the information to develop the original profile and who would liaise with Speedwing to implement the new training programme. Speedwing was able to use the information in the database to develop a customised training plan for each travel agency branch and to mail only training information that was relevant to each branch's needs. It also enabled Speedwing to build a training partnership with the travel agencies and use that partnership to improve the quality of service available to British Airways customers.

COMMUNICATING TRAINING

Working with local outlets to identify their training needs and tailor courses to their requirements is an essential stage in making the best use of local skills. However, it is also important to communicate the scope and importance of training to local outlets to ensure that they participate in training programmes. Communications should be aimed at:

- the senior manager;
- departmental manager;
- trainees;
- training specialist.

Senior managers

Since it is the senior managers within local outlets who control the funds available for training, training should be positioned as an essential investment in the future success and profitability of the organisation. Training is not perceived as a current expense but as a long-term business investment. It is also an investment that will result in improved customer service and better staff relations – intangibles that make a major contribution to the business but are not easily quantified. It is important to stress how skills development helps to improve the local outlet's competitive ability and provides it with a clear growth path to meet future business objectives and deal with rapid changes in the marketplace. Senior managers in the local outlet do not need to know the details of training programmes, they need to understand the contribution they will make to the business.

Departmental managers

Departmental managers are under increasing pressure to produce better and better results or to increase output and production with fewer and fewer resources. Training can help to improve staff performance and help to relieve some of those pressures. However the training must be seen as relevant and it must be positioned as helping to overcome day-to-day problems. Training should also be convenient and practical. Although most departmental managers understand the long-term benefits of training, they may be loathe to release key staff for even short periods of time when they are under pressure to achieve results. The training proposals must be convenient, not time-consuming and promise improved practical results that will lead to short- and long-term departmental improvements.

Trainees

Trainees need to know that they play a vital role within the organisation and that their contribution is valued. Training will help to improve their personal skills and ensure that they can continue to make an increasing contribution and deal confidently with the problems of an increasingly complex, rapidly changing market. Trainees also need to understand why their skills need to be improved and how the new skills will help them improve service to customers. By demonstrating the change in customer needs through surveys and customer comments, the company can demonstrate what customers expect and want from staff at every level.

Training specialists

Training specialists within local outlets also need to be kept up to date with training developments; they are responsible for identifying training needs and organising the courses. The supplier's training programme should be positioned as a valuable addition to the resources they have available.

Training options

Convenience and relevance were identified as key messages to trainees and their managers. There is a pressure on time and funds which can act as a barrier to an effective programme of local training. Suppliers should therefore look carefully at the way they deliver training so that they can provide the greatest benefits with the least inconvenience.

There are a number of options.

● Companies with large branch or distributor networks may run central training centres for technical, management or sales training.

- Local or distance-learning options, to improve the reach and effectiveness of the training budgets.
- Video has been used as support or substitute for face-to-face training. While there are many excellent general-purpose training videos, they lack the specific content and the capacity to be tailored to local needs.
- Corporate video and television networks can be used to relay information around an organisation and provide a tailored information in very sophisticated networks. Although their primary role is to improve internal communications and provide up-to-date management information in a convenient format, the networks can also be used to broadcast training material, product information and market information which can be integrated with a branch training programme.
- Interactive video takes video a stage nearer to personalised training by providing a training resource that can be tailored to an individual's own rate of progress.
- Companies that do not have the funds to invest in sophisticated training technology have also used correspondence courses to train staff who are too far from training centres to take advantage of the facilities.

An international engineering company with a worldwide distributor network used a correspondence course produced in ten languages to improve product and application knowledge among distributor sales and service staff. The course, which consists of 30 separate modules, was extremely popular and was adopted by a number of international engineering colleges as a basic course for residential students. Although correspondence courses may seem extremely basic in relation to other training techniques, they have been proved extremely effective and they may form a growing part of the return to self-study methods.

Recent developments in management training indicate that self-study will become increasingly important. The National Vocational Qualification (NVQ) programme, which seeks to improve the competence of middle and junior managers uses an integrated set of practical on-the-job training, short workshops, workbooks and reference books to enable managers to improve their competence against a range of disciplines needed for success in general management. Managers follow a series of courses that develop core skills and which are directly related to the tasks they carry out. NVQs can be used to develop general management competence within the local network and can complement the more specific market-based training offered by training specialists.

Many organisations, conscious of the problems their branches face in releasing staff to go on courses, are taking training to the branches. ICL, for example, operated a programme called the SkillsVan which transported training resources around the country to different ICL branches and contained all the material needed to operate a wide range of training programmes.

Ford ran a Dealer Training service which developed and delivered customised training courses for individual dealerships. The programme consisted of a training assessment followed by a review of training needs and a specified number of days training per month to enhance key skills within the dealership. These training options are helping to make training more convenient within the branch and raise the standards of customer service throughout a branch network.

CONCENTRATING RESOURCES IN CENTRES OF EXCELLENCE

An alternative to running large-scale local training programmes is to take certain highly-skilled tasks out of the local outlet and move them into centres of excellence. These are most likely to be tasks that require scarce skills that are not available in every branch. By putting together skilled people in centres of excellence and making them available to customers throughout the country, a supplier can offer a consistent level of service everywhere.

Earlier in this chapter, we discussed the role of the ICL Customer Reception Centre in improving the quality of response to customer queries. The Customer Reception Centre was part of an overall strategy which included the development of centres of excellence and the introduction of sophisticated service tools and databases. Hand-held terminals, for example, are now used in a number of different industries to carry out service diagnosis and to retrieve and access service information. Service engineers can key in fault symptoms and compare the problems they have found with known faults recorded on the service database. They also use the terminals to log details of a current fault so that the main service database can be updated. Tools like this ensure that locally-based service engineers can deliver an increasingly consistent standard of service without investing in major training programmes.

UTILISING BEST PRACTICE

To help build team spirit within a local network and to improve overall performance and consistency, suppliers are encouraging their outlets to participate in developing standards by sharing examples of best practice.

In an earlier chapter, we gave the example of Johnson Controls, an international components manufacturer, which utilised international teams to help develop the best possible solution when it was opening a new plant. Teams from plants in other territories would work together to identify opportunities to use best practice in the new plant and also to highlight any potential risks.

The Arlington Motor Company used a similar method to introduce consistent standards into a disparate group of car dealerships. It realised that the performance of individual outlets was, to a certain extent, determined by the skills and attitudes of the dealer principal. The head-office team identified the critical performance factors and established benchmarks for each factor. However, rather than impose common standards on the local outlets, the head-office team decided to introduce change through participation.

It identified 'star performers' within the network, and invited them to a hotel to work for a week with an independent consultant and share their experiences. By the end of the week, the group had prepared a proposal for best practice within each of the group's operating activities – car sales, commercial vehicles, leasing, parts, service and fleet business. The draft proposals were circulated to management teams within each outlet for comment and suggestion and the result was a set of group operating standards that were acceptable throughout the network. By concentrating on the most important factors and achieving a high level of participation, the group was able to deal with the problem of 'performance scatter' in a large, semi-independent network.

ACHIEVING CONSISTENT VISUAL STANDARDS

It is not only quality standards that need to be consistent. Visual identity is a critical element in signalling to customers and the local network that the company means business, and a new corporate identity is an opportunity to introduce new standards of performance.

Corporate identity is the term given to the visual appearance of a company. It includes:

- the colours;
- the company logo;
- typeface;
- uniforms;
- appearance of retail outlets;
- visual standards imposed on brochures, advertisements and other communications material.

A corporate identity should ideally reflect what the company stands for in terms of quality and direction. A good corporate identity is timeless and is carefully guarded by its owners. Over a period of time, the corporate identities of organisations like IBM, Shell, BP and Ford have evolved in minute detail, but are clearly related to the original identity. The identities of organisations like British Telecom and British Airways, on the other hand, have changed more radically to reflect new corporate values and directions. Both sets of identities have succeeded in achieving an important communications task for their owners and both have helped to build a reputation for excellence and achievement.

Companies maintain the strength of their identity by implementing it across every form of visual communication and ensuring that the identity is used consistently on every occasion. It is particularly important for organisations whose activities are diverse or geographically spread that their total strength should be recognised. This also gives the constituent units within a large organisation a sense of belonging to a team.

Corporate identity is therefore an essential element in local marketing support. It provides the opportunity to impose a consistent appearance on each outlet in the network so that customers immediately recognise the outlet, and it enables a brand identity to be built around the network.

Consistent appearance

The most important aspect of corporate identity is that it imposes a consistent visual appearance and standard on each outlet and ensures that the corporate reputation is communicated effectively. Corporate identity does not just impose consistency for the sake of consistency, the corporate standards have been carefully designed to reflect customers' needs and the quality of service available.

When George Davis and the David Davis consultancy developed the original identity for the Next retail chain, the identity was designed to reflect a certain consumer lifestyle and to provide an efficient, cost-effective method of displaying the company's merchandise.

Motorists on the move are attracted by the competing signage of BP, Shell, Esso, Gulf, Fina and a host of other national and regional petrol companies. By linking a strong corporate identity to high standards of customer service, any one of these signs should ensure that the customers will immediately be aware of the whole service on offer. The use of corporate identity has become even more complicated now that petrol stations have been transformed into roadside retail outlets catering for motorists and local residents. The identity of a petrol station no longer signals just the name of a company, but the promise of a certain standard of service.

Consistency is more important when the outlets are not part of a franchised network, but are independent outlets who may be operating multiple franchises. Although it is difficult to impose an overall identity on an outlet like this, the use of selected elements such as signage or the use of corporate colours or a logo on the building or on distributor communications material can help to maintain recognition levels and ensure that customers understand the benefits of dealing with that outlet.

Scope of corporate identity

Corporate identity is a wide-ranging activity and there are a number of good books on the subject. In its purest sense, corporate identity covers the visual appearance of a company and designers will create an entire system which looks at every aspect of a company's operations.

Although corporate identity is essentially a visual study, it requires the close working involvement of the senior management team because the impact of a new corporate identity can have a fundamental effect on the perception and prospects of a company. A corporate identity reflects a company's strengths and its future direction and it should be planned carefully, whether it is a complete departure from the existing identity or simply a redesign to bring the company's visual style up to date.

In terms of a local support programme, there are a number of important considerations.

- Does the nature of the network allow a complete identity to be imposed or can it be only partial identity change?
- What is the scale of the change in terms of physical work, resources and time?
- How can a new identity be used to improve local marketing performance?
- Should the identity be flexible enough to take account of national, regional or local marketing differences, or should it be a rigid system that achieves complete uniformity?
- Will the identity be applied only to key outlets within the network or will it be applied universally?

- Can the identity be controlled at local level and how will the identity team maintain standards?

These are general questions that the identity team will consider before they begin the design process. When they have an agreed identity and a system for implementing it, the identity will have to be applied to a wide range of items within the distributor network. These include:

- signage – overall external signage for the outlets and the signs for internal departments;
- display and merchandising material within the retail areas in a local outlet – shelf signs, merchandising units, posters, pricing systems, product information and other point-of-sale material;
- staff uniforms, company ties and other workwear;
- style and treatment of the interior and exterior of the building, including layout of showroom, retail areas, customer reception areas and other customer facilities;
- design of stationery, literature, direct mail and other communications material to achieve high levels of consistency.

The scope of corporate identity is far reaching and its major benefit is that it imposes a level of consistency on a local network which ensures immediate recognition by customers. However, there are many other benefits.

- An effective corporate identity can build a sense of team spirit within the entire network and across individual outlets.
- A new corporate identity has an extremely high profile and the publicity it attracts can help to raise awareness of the direction the company and the whole network is going in.
- A high-quality corporate identity, which raises a great deal of publicity and customer interest, can help to boost morale and create pride in working for the network.
- The identity can also enhance the status and perception of individual outlets, helping to boost business by attracting new customers or confirming relationships with existing customers.
- It can improve the quality of merchandising within an outlet by

creating a more attractive sales environment that clearly directs customers to the right sales areas and presents products and services effectively.

- It gives suppliers the opportunity to re-evaluate their standards of service and the fundamental nature of the business, and this may encourage them to aim for even higher standards to take advantage of the new identity.

Planning

It is very easy to regard a new corporate identity as a means of transforming the culture and perception of an organisation, but unless the organisation itself can reflect the promise of the new identity, it will be wasted. A glossy identity on a poor organisation has been described as papering over the cracks and will achieve only a short-term benefit. Developing a new identity should be integrated with a fundamental review of all the company's activities and the development of a corporate plan that ensures that every activity that impacts on customer satisfaction is optimised.

In the context of local marketing operations, corporate identity would be integrated with staff training, improvement of customer-facing facilities, development of systems that improve efficiency and customer service, and the development of an attitude of customer care.

The planning process must therefore begin with an assessment of the strengths and weaknesses of the local network.

- How do customers see the local network;
- What are their attitudes?
- What would they like to see improved?
- Is the local outlet seen as progressive, traditional, innovative, service-oriented?
- How does the local outlet view the supplier or the head office:
  - is it supportive?
  - does it offer good prospects for the future?
  - does it work in partnership with the local outlets?
  - does it suggest a company with a future?

- How well is the current identity perceived?
- Is it immediately recognisable?
- Is it liked by customers?
- Is it confused with any other organisation?
- Does the current identity have strengths which should be retained or should there be a complete rethink?

This kind of analysis may require wide-ranging discussions between the identity design consultancy, company management, local management, customers and other interested parties to build a complete picture of the present situation. The consultancy can then set objectives for the new identity that will enable its proposals to be evaluated objectively. The objectives that relate to the local network might include:

- ensure a consistent identity for all franchised outlets;
- strongly brand independent multi-franchise outlets;
- develop a flexible identity that will accommodate regional variations across an international network;
- develop a cost-effective system that can be implemented in a short time scale with minimal disruption to normal trading;
- build on the strengths of the existing identity, which is shown by research to be highly regarded;
- bring the identity up to date and reduce the confusion with any other visual symbol.

The consultancy can develop a series of proposals for the new identity and demonstrate how it will operate within the network. These proposals would normally take the form of a written plan, together with sketches of the new logo and a series of examples of the new identity in operation.

IMPLEMENTATION

The planning process would also include a detailed proposal for implementing the programme, including a timetable, indication of costs and resources required, inclusion of any pilot scheme and the key dates for progress of the programme. When the initial design proposals have been accepted, the company has the basis of its corporate identity and it can carry out the detailed design of all the elements listed in the section 'the scope of corporate identity'. The detailed design would proceed through two stages – generic design of the items in the identity programme and detailed design to suit the implementation on different sites. The design and implementation can be handled in a number of different ways.

- Using a corporate-identity consultancy or architectural practice specialising in this type of activity. They prepare the consultation document, initial proposals and detailed designs, and may manage the overall implementation using approved suppliers or sub-contractors. They charge a professional fee for the design and development stages, and they would charge the production and implementation costs at cost, plus a management fee for super-vising the implementation, or a total cost which included their mark-up on suppliers' costs.
- A company with design and programme-management resources can handle the consultation and design stages internally and use the same sub-contractors and suppliers to implement the programme. However, staff must have a breadth of experience of corporate identity to handle complex projects and provide the objective viewpoint that is so essential. A small number of companies have recruited independent professional designers as consultants to their board and used them in the same way as staff on an ongoing basis.
- Use the services of a shopfitting company or other company sup-plying the corporate identity elements; they would provide design services to handle relatively simple identity changes, but would be unlikely to provide the high-level consultancy that is an integral element of effective corporate identity. They would provide a packaged service which might include an element of design.

The implementation of a new corporate identity across a local network can have far-reaching consequences and many companies carry out pilot projects to assess the feasibility of the project and to get initial feedback to the changes from local outlets, staff and customers. For example, they might choose a single site which is geographically convenient or they might choose a high-profile outlet which can act as the flagship for the rest of the network and attract high levels of interest and response. A pilot programme proves whether a corporate identity programme is practical and effective, and ensures that any essential modifications can be built in.

The national or international implementation must be carefully planned to achieve maximum impact and a cost-effective solution. A company that wants to transform its identity in a day or over a weekend, for example, must ensure that all the elements are in position and that it has sufficient resources to carry out a simultaneous transformation at each of its sites. The alternative is to implement the programme in phases, with a set number of branches upgraded at one time and the whole network completed within a set timeframe. The phased implementation has less pressure built into it, but both approaches require considerable planning and co-ordination to ensure that the programmes are completed on target. Delays not only disrupt business, but they also have an impact on the company credibility as delay is seen as a failure. To avoid disruption, many corporate identity implementations are carried out over a weekend or during periods of low business so that customers are not affected.

Launching a new identity

The introduction of a new identity does not just depend on successful implementation, it takes an effective launch to the local outlets to ensure that they accept it and understand their role in the transfer. The launch can be handled in a number of ways:

- by holding a national launch event attended by key people from the local network. They are given a presentation on the new identity and practical guidelines on its implementation;
- local outlets receive a launch guide which provides a full explanation of the changes together with the procedures for implementation;

- a presentation at the individual outlet to explain the detailed implementation of the programme.

If the presentation is not handled effectively, the local outlets will not give the programme their full commitment, and they may not carry out all the critical activities that ensure success. The launch should cover the following areas:

- why the new identity has been developed and the benefits it will bring;
- the cost implications of the new identity and how it will provide cost-effective solutions to current problems;
- the scope of the new identity and how it will be applied to the local outlet;
- an indication of the appearance of the local outlet when the new identity has been applied;
- the timetable and procedure for implementation;
- the support that will be provided and the local outlet's responsibilities;
- the programme for managing the identity locally;
- the public relations activities that will be used to explain the benefits of the new identity to customers at national and local levels.

This presentation is likely to be given to the local management team but it may need further support to launch the programme to its staff and customers. As the remainder of this chapter shows, it is important that the programme is introduced and accepted at every level because it can make an important contribution to customer satisfaction. The launch of a new identity can be subject to misinterpretation by people who believe it is an unnecessary extravagance; some of the high-profile companies that provide a public service and have introduced a radical new identity have come under criticism from members of the public who have not understood the strategic importance of the change. The launch also provides an important opportunity to promote the new direction the company is taking and it is crucial that the launch is successful.

Local implementation

An identity that is national or international may not be suitable for every outlet in the network. In the international network it may be necessary to adjust to national differences. To ensure that the identity benefits every territory, it is necessary to carry out detailed consultation with the regions and the supplier simply issues guidelines and instructions for local manufacture and implementation.

When Motorcraft, the automotive components manufacturer, developed a new identity for its parts and accessories packaging, it had to make provision for local manufacture of a number of products in the range. Many of the products could be sourced centrally but others had to comply with local legislation or product variations. A comprehensive guide was produced to provide national sales companies with detailed guidelines on the design standards and the manufacturing specifications for each item in the range. This part of the guide covered:

- design standards;
- dimensions;
- corporate colours;
- typeface;
- use of the logo;
- position of type and clarity of message;
- use of illustration or photography;
- the material to be used in local production;
- the quality standards to be imposed on local manufacturers.

The guide also contains detailed instructions on how to use the standard guide to brief local suppliers and where to get support and advice to achieve the best possible result. If a company is using other sources to achieve local implementation, it must ensure that the design proposals are flexible enough to cope with local variations in production standards and it must provide an advisory service to deal with production queries and with questions about variations to overall standards.

The same points apply if a supplier is carrying out a transformation of all the interiors and exteriors of distributor outlets and is using local sub-contractors. The sub-contractors need to have detailed guidelines on implementation and ideally will conform to approved quality standards so that the whole process is carried out consistently.

Staff training

It is not sufficient to impose a new identity on a local network without explanation and without ensuring that staff understand the implications for organisational performance. A new corporate identity must be accompanied by the highest standards of customer care and by remedial action in other areas of corporate weakness. A new identity is an opportunity for staff to reassess the standards they offer and it provides visible evidence of their commitment to change.

Part of the identity implementation process must therefore be a training programme that explains what the new identity is supposed to convey and how that converts to practical actions in the local outlet. For example, if the identity conveys an innovative, market-focused organisation that is dedicated to the highest standards of customer care, it is vital that staff actually achieve this. Poor customer service, old-fashioned methods of business and administrative efficiency can ruin the effect of any identity.

When Case Europe introduced a new retail-led identity into its European parts network, it wanted to convert the network from local warehouses to proactive market-led retail centres that would succeed through quality of service. As well as developing a new merchandising system and a new signage system, it introduced a new range of fast-moving products that would be suitable for a self-service outlet. To ensure that local staff would be able to take advantage of the new marketing opportunities, the company ran courses on retail techniques which included product display, stockholding, customer service and merchandising.

Programme management

A corporate identity programme requires strong management to make it work efficiently. The programme must be managed to ensure that it meets its initial implementation targets – on time, on budget and to the levels of quality expected, and it must also continue to deliver the business benefits that were set for it. The head-office management team must ensure that each of the local implementations conforms to national standards and that any variants fit within the overall guidelines. The head-office team must also set up local management teams to ensure that the identity is implemented and maintained successfully. Local managers would be responsible for achieving the overall standards within their branch and for operating any training programmes that might be relevant.

Programme maintenance

The test of a good corporate identity is whether it can survive in use after the initial implementation.

- Is it timeless enough or will it become outdated quickly when design fashions change?
- Is it flexible enough to accommodate local or detailed changes without losing the impact of the whole programme?
- Are the guidelines sufficiently clear to ensure consistent implementation of all aspects of the programme?
- Can the programme be refreshed or updated regularly without losing the impact of the original identity?

Maintaining the strength of a corporate identity is one of the most important activities, because people within a group instinctively want to make small changes to customise the identity to their own requirements. Using the logo in a different position, varying the corporate colour or typeface because the printer didn't happen to have the right colour in stock, using the logo as a name rather than a graphic element, using inferior materials to save money or simply ignoring the guidelines altogether are some of the more common problems faced by companies that are trying to manage an identity and achieve consistency. Adhering to consistent standards requires persuasion rather than rigid rules but, provided people understand why it is important to be consistent, they will find it easier to conform.

SUMMARY

This chapter describes one of the major problems faced by companies marketing through multiple outlets – how to ensure that customers receive the same standard of service in every branch. It shows how consistency can be used as a basis for branding local outlets in the same way as products. The chapter describes how quality standards such as BS 5750 are used increasingly at local level to measure and monitor performance in line with agreed standards. Staff skills are a key element of consistent performance and the chapter shows how local skills profiles are used to develop targeted training programmes. It is essential to communicate the benefits of training to local management and staff and to offer them flexible training options. The chapter provides examples of this and shows how some organisations deal with the problem of performance scatter by concentrating resources in centres of excellence or by utilising best practice from around their networks. The second part of the chapter provides detailed guidelines on achieving consistent visual standards, explaining the scope of corporate-identity programmes and showing how to plan, implement and maintain them to achieve high standards of visual consistency.

ACTION CHECKLIST

BRANDING

How important is consistency to your network?
Do you brand your network in the same way as your products?

Could international branding reflect local customer expectations?

Do you have the resources to establish international brand awareness?

What are the brand values of your network and how well do they reflect customer expectations?

Is it important that you transfer existing brand values to new outlets?

QUALITY

Can you apply measurable quality standards to your network?

Which processes would you apply quality to?

Do quality standards vary across your international networks?

Can you apply international quality standards to your local outlets?

Is it practicable to register your network under an independent quality scheme?

How do you measure your local customers' views of quality?

Do you utilise customer response to improve quality standards?

SKILLS

Do your local outlets understand the importance of training and do they have effective training programmes in position?

Which skills are crucial to consistent performance throughout your network?

Can you utilise different training options to ensure that the critical skills are developed?

Could you take certain critical skilled activities out of local outlets into centres of excellence?

Are you encouraging your outlets to share best practice with the rest of the network?

VISUAL STANDARDS

Do you have a strong corporate identity and is it used consistently throughout the network?

Have you evaluated local customer perceptions of your corporate identity and do they reflect the right values?

Is your corporate identity flexible enough to be used throughout your international network?

If you have to use local suppliers to implement an international corporate identity, can you control local standards?

Do your local outlets have clear guidelines on using corporate identity?

Is the strength of your corporate identity being eroded by inconsistent local use?

Can you control the use of the corporate identity more effectively?

9

FOCUS ON CUSTOMER CARE

INTRODUCTION

Customer care has become one of the most important issues facing businesses in every market. Customer care programmes come under a number of different titles – customer service, customer satisfaction, customer focus, customer-oriented. Their common theme is meeting the customers' requirements and ensuring that all aspects of the business contribute to customer satisfaction. The intention is to build repeat business. If customers are satisfied with the product and the standards of service they receive, they will return to the same outlet again and again for major or minor purchases.

Most companies are now operating a customer care programme of some description, but the problems of running a successful programme are multiplied when the same programme is operated through local outlets. Inconsistent customer care performance can have a negative effect on customer perceptions. Petrol companies, for example, know that every time a customer walks into one of their outlets, wherever they are in the country, they should expect to receive the same standards of service. Nationwide consistency is essential when customers are likely to visit multiple outlets – one poor performance can threaten the customer's perception of the entire operation. However, the same principle should be applied to multi-site opportunities even when customers are likely to use only one site.

Customer care has two aspects:

- the physical means of delivering customer service;
- the attitude of staff.

A company wishing to improve its standards of customer care could set up a customer care hotline to handle queries or complaints – that would be the physical part of the equation; but if the staff who manned the hotline were unsympathetic, the customer care benefit could be lost. Anyone who wishes to implement an effective customer care strategy should look for a balance between the two. It is also important to recognise that management and staff at every level in the local outlet affect customer care and loyalty. Programmes that build a customer care attitude must operate at every level. Customer care can operate in a variety of ways:

- offering customers the products and services that reflect their real needs;
- offering greater levels of convenience which make it easier for customers to buy from your local outlets;
- providing a customer service centre where customers can make enquiries or complain;
- improving the overall quality of service so that customers recognise a change in performance.

The most important aspect of any programme is to focus people on customer care and this can be achieved in a number of ways:

- running customer focus panels to identify customer needs and discuss their views on the quality of service;
- issuing customer focus standards to ensure consistent standards;
- introducing customer care programmes that give a high profile to the whole process of customer care;
- running customer care programmes to ensure that all staff understand the importance of customer care;
- introducing customer satisfaction ratings to measure how well local outlets are performing;
- operating customer satisfaction incentive schemes to reward outlets that have achieved the highest levels of customer satisfaction;
- integrating customer care activities into business and marketing programmes to ensure that the whole business is driven by customer needs;
- using customer care to build customer loyalty.

The remainder of this chapter describes each of these actions in more detail; however the subject of customer care is broad and is covered in *Total Customer Satisfaction* by Jacques Horovitz and Michele Jurgens Panak in the Pitman Financial Times series and in Ian Linton's book for the Pitman Institute of Management series, *Building Customer Loyalty*.

CUSTOMER FOCUS PANELS

It would be very easy to introduce customer care slogans and encourage staff to demonstrate customer care, but the actions would be wasted without an understanding of what customers actually needed. As so many observers have pointed out, 'Customer care is more than wearing a smile and saying "have a nice day".' Customer care is meeting customers' real needs and the hardest part is to identify those needs.

One way is to use a technique known as focus panels where customers and an interviewer meet to discuss their requirements and attitudes to the service that is offered. Eaton House Consultants runs a number of customer focus panels for major petrol retailers. The customers in this case are motorists and they include a cross-section of a petrol station's customer base:

- business travellers;
- delivery drivers;
- long-distance lorry drivers;
- domestic drivers;
- elderly drivers;
- handicapped drivers.

The aim was to find out what each of these motorists wanted from a petrol service station. The key issues were convenience of opening hours, ease of access, number of pumps, location, payment facilities, customer facilities such as toilets and drinks, and the availability of other products such as snacks, motoring products and, increasingly, the range of other products available in the forecourt. The information provided by the motorists' panel showed the retailer the direction in which it could expand its business and provided a valuable indication of the areas that needed improvement.

The second stage of the focus panel was to review the findings of the panel with the management team and to develop an action plan to make any improvements that had been identified as necessary. The information was also used as a basis for national planning. By putting together the information from panels around the country, the head-office team was able to identify regional and national patterns in consumer requirements. This provided a valuable basis for planning national forecourt-development programmes and providing the right level of regional and local support. The focus panels were held on a regional basis and this proved a valuable method of monitoring customers' response to the improvements that had been made at the suggestion of earlier focus panels. By showing that it was prepared to respond to motorists' concerns, the retailer was able to demonstrate high levels of customer care.

This particular programme enabled detailed customer focus programmes to be developed at local level and integrated with national customer focus programmes. The research programme carried out by Glen Carter Associates for a European automotive components manufacturer shows how the same principles can be applied at a pan-European level. Comments from customers given in a separate survey showed that they were having difficulty in obtaining information from dealers on the company's range of accessories. When they were able to obtain copies of the accessories catalogue, customers found them difficult to use and, as a result, their overall levels of satisfaction were reduced. The research also indicated that the response to the accessories catalogue varied by location.

As the accessories programme was an important factor in maintaining contact between vehicle sales, the company decided to commission more detailed research into the customers' requirements for an accessories catalogue. The researchers decided to concentrate on two main questions.

- How easy did customers find it to get information on accessories?
- What sort of information did they need?

On the question of getting information, customers commented that they had to ask for catalogues and, where they were on display, they were uncertain whether they had to pay for them. Commenting on the contents of the catalogue, customers were divided over the question of whether accessories should be shown by model; many felt that prices should be shown and most were confused about the process of ordering accessories. Customers were also shown competitive accessories literature and asked for their response to content and quality. The research programme was carried out across seven European countries and the results, unsurprisingly, revealed significant differences between markets. The company's response was to develop a series of accessories brochures incorporating local variations. The brochures were initially produced by model range with a simple ordering system based on product numbers. Each of the seventeen language variations contained model information that was specific to that territory. Prices were included or omitted depending on the response of the local market and the views of dealers in that territory. The content of the brochure was now tailored more closely to the needs of customers in each market.

To ensure that customers were able to obtain the information easily within dealerships, the company developed a merchandising and incentive programme which included prominent displays for the customer, direct mail aimed at local customers and a structured incentive programme based on sales of accessories. As a result of this customer research, the company was able to introduce an accessories programme that reflected customer needs as well as the specific needs of local markets.

CUSTOMER FOCUS STANDARDS

Using focus panels is a good way to build an understanding of customer needs. If that understanding can be built into customer focus standards that determine how the business is run at a local level, that will help to improve the consistency of performance and demonstrate to customers that the company is responding to their requirements. Many franchised and independent distributors have to conform to operating requirements as part of their distributor agreement. Typically, these would cover the size of the premises, facilities, stock levels, head count, capital funding, management skills and training requirements to ensure that the branch was able to provide the level of service covered by its agreement.

An increasing number of companies are introducing customer focus standards as part of their agreement to improve levels of customer satisfaction. The Post Office, for example, is moving many of its main post offices from central high-street positions to new locations within large retail outlets or to out-of-town shopping centres. Part of the reason for the change is to reduce the cost of maintaining an expensive town-centre position, but the Post Office is also taking the opportunity to move to premises that are more convenient for its customers and to improve the quality of service.

Many were relocated within retail outlets and were able to offer their customers longer opening hours, plus the convenience of the chance to do other shopping at the same time. The out-of-town locations were even more convenient with adequate parking, wheelchair access, spacious premises and the same benefits of longer opening hours and one-stop shopping. These retailing developments, together with future developments in counter automation, training and an increasing range of products and services were at the heart of the Post Office's drive to become a more customer-focused organisation serving the needs of the local market.

A number of American-style pizza home-delivery services are run as franchise operations and they aim to improve the quality and consistency of their service by introducing customer focus standards. They realise that, in a fiercely competitive market, they have to establish a strong brand identity and that identity is based not just on the quality of the pizza but on the quality of service. Many of the operators offer a guaranteed home-delivery time backed by a full refund if they fail to meet the time. They want to attract customers by offering the convenience of home delivery, but they have suffered in the past from inconsistent delivery performance with the pizzas arriving unacceptably late or arriving cold. The promise to deliver on time or provide a refund is a powerful motivator for the local staff since failure hits directly at their profit levels.

Direct Line Insurance has introduced high levels of convenience and rapid response into the car insurance market and shows that a successful and profitable business can be built on customer focus standards. The company accepts enquiries through a well-trained customer reception centre. The customers are guided through a series of simple questions and the respondent then provides an immediate quotation. If the customer wishes to proceed, the respondent issues immediate cover without any further administration or form filling. Claims are handled in a similar way. The result for the customer is a service that is simple, responsive, convenient and good value for money. Direct Line has the advantage that it handles incoming enquiries centrally, but other organisations can use the same principles to establish a customer-focused service.

CUSTOMER CARE PROGRAMMES

Customer care programmes provide local outlets with the physical means to improve customer care performance. They are the 'material' aspect of customer care performance described at the beginning of this chapter, and local outlets are encouraged or obliged to participate in the programmes.

For example, most car manufacturers now offer a courtesy vehicle service to their service customers. Research identified that convenience was the biggest factor in selecting a service outlet. Many motorists felt that they could not do without some form of transport. Service centres that were located near homes, places of work or public transport routes were appealing to customers and car dealers that could not offer similar levels of convenience were losing business. Some car dealers offered their customers lower price car rental when their vehicles were in for repair, but this still represented an additional cost and was a poor alternative.

Manufacturers introduced the concept of courtesy vehicles and set up fleets at dealerships around the country. The service was optional and dealers were encouraged to offer the vehicles to customers who were likely to suffer the most inconvenience as a result of their cars being off the road. The programme operating guide identified these as business users, doctors, nurses, mothers with young children and others. The intention was that the courtesy vehicle was a discretionary offer and not an automatic offer with every service. The customer should recognise that the dealership was making a genuine attempt to reduce inconvenience and offer greater standards of customer care.

Homebuilders, recognising that customers may have concerns about the quality of their new homes, have introduced customer care visits at set periods after the customers have moved in. The customer care visits give customers the opportunity to discuss any queries or problems they might have about their new homes. The programme allows the company to take the initiative and defuse any potentially damaging complaints. This only works if the homebuilders implement a quality building programme and are prepared to carry out remedial work without fuss. Putting right defective work is not in itself a customer care programme, but taking positive steps to offer a proactive response is. If the programme succeeds, customers will perceive that the homebuilder is a caring company and is prepared to respond to customer needs. This is an important form of local marketing support because it brands the homebuilder and, when customers move, they will be encouraged to buy another house from the same builder. Given that householders may move on average every five years, the customer care programme is an important factor in customer loyalty.

CUSTOMER CARE TRAINING

The second part of the customer care equation is attitude – ensuring that local staff are committed to the highest standards of customer care. The customer care training industry is now highly developed and there is a wide variety of general-purpose and tailored training programmes available. Videos such as the Video Arts series have established an excellent reputation for their programmes on caring for the customer. The Sunday Times publishes videos and books on customer care and there are numerous conferences and training organisations offering individual programmes. The problem is not in obtaining training material, but knowing how to apply it.

Ford has renamed its Technical Training Centre the Ford Care Institute because this reflects the central role that customer care plays at every level in the industry. Technicians who service cars were not traditionally regarded as contributors to customer care but, if they did a poor job this reflected on customer satisfaction. Included in the technical training programmes were modules on cleanliness of the vehicle, checking workmanship, using protective covers to prevent grease marks, and tips on returning the vehicle in the condition it arrived, with seats and mirrors in the same position, radio tuned to the correct frequency, ashtrays emptied and, most important, the car working properly.

An increasing number of companies recognise the contribution that good administration makes to effective customer relations and they are training their staff in the virtues of accurate invoicing. Accurate invoicing obviously helps the company's own cashflow by reducing the number of errors and speeding up payment, but it also helps to reduce customers' administration burden in checking and querying invoices. A supplier can provide material and personal support to local outlets to ensure that the same standards are maintained. It can issue material support in the form of standard accounting packages and procedures and it can provide training in the importance and techniques of accurate invoicing.

It's just as important to train the managers and supervisors of staff responsible for customer care so that they are prepared to commit time and resources to training. When British Airways launched its long-term programme to improve the quality of customer service before privatisation, it introduced a comprehensive management training programme before it began training the people who delivered the customer service in the front line. It was essential, they believed, that managers should understand the problems customer service staff faced and provide them with the proper levels of support.

CUSTOMER SATISFACTION RATINGS

Customer care is a business discipline that can be managed and measured. It ensures that the company can retain customers and ensure future income and profitability. In terms of customer care performance, the customer satisfaction index is the most efficient method of measuring achievement and improvement. A customer satisfaction index takes the results from a number of satisfaction surveys and allocates a numerical value to key customer satisfaction indicators. A local outlet is then given an overall index of performance which can be compared with other branches and measured on a year-on-year basis. Customer satisfaction ratings are a direct method of assessing customer care performance and they provide a means for motivating branches to improve customer care standards.

The basis of customer satisfaction ratings is a customer satisfaction survey. This is sent at intervals to customers who have purchased a product or service, a week or a month after purchase, for example, and six months or a year after initial purchase. The first questionnaire is to establish the customer's response to the way the sale was handled, and the second to establish how the customer feels about the product or service in use and how they feel about the aftercare they have received from the outlet. The questionnaire asks customers to respond to questions with a scale of satisfaction – fully satisfied, very satisfied, satisfied, not very satisfied, very dissatisfied – or alternatively asked to respond on a numerical scale, 'on a scale of 1–10, how satisfied were you with . . . 1 is very dissatisfied, 10 is very satisfied'. Customers can also provide written comments on aspects of the service and, in some cases, ask for specific actions such as an explanation from the departmental manager.

A first-stage questionnaire might include such questions as:

'How satisfied are you with:
- the response of sales store;
- the location and convenience of the staff;
- convenience of opening hours;
- ease of parking;
- availability of product information;

- product knowledge of staff;
- waiting time to be served;
- choice of payment methods;
- explanation of options;
- presentation of product;
- availability of finance;
- explanation of aftercare?'

The questionnaire that followed up at six months or a year after purchase would focus on customer satisfaction with the product or service and the quality of aftercare. It might include questions such as:

'How satisifed are you with:
- the quality and performance of the product;
- the reliability of the product;
- the benefits of the service;
- the standard of the service;
- the response of the branch to any queries;
- the value of any instruction manuals;
- the quality of aftercare service;
- the value of the warranty;
- availability of replacement parts;
- flexibility of service plans;
- availability of accessories?'

The two types of questionnaire are designed to assess how much effort the local outlet is putting into selling the product properly; i.e. does the customer believe the outlet is trying to help him select the right product. The answers to the questions can be used to assess the performance of the salesforce and the quality of product information. The questions on convenience can also act as a guide to the convenience of the store and help to plan changes or improvements.

The second questionnaire seeks to find out how well the outlet is faring during the critical period after the sale. It reminds the customer that there is life after the sale and helps to build contact during the critical period between sales when the customer could easily be influenced by offers from another manufacturer. If the customer is satisfied with all aspects of the outlet's service – product, convenience, quality and aftercare – it is likely that the customer will return to that outlet for the next purchase.

If customers do not indicate satisfaction, the outlet has an opportunity to take remedial action or to respond to their customer's concerns. The real importance of a customer satisfaction index is whether it generates action and improves business performance. The index must be carefully weighted to focus the attention of the local outlet on the key indicators of customer satisfaction. Each response is given a score and the totals of all customer responses are added up to give an overall index for the outlet. The index may be based on the answers to all questions or it may be based on a selection of those questions that are most important to overall satisfaction.

Car dealerships, for example, concentrate on the response to aftercare – 'How satisfied were you with the service from the Parts and Service departments?' – because they know that the key to retaining customers between new-car sales is the two- to three- year period when the customer deals with the Parts and Service departments. One European manufacturer calculated that the new-car sales process generated a possible one million contacts per year, while aftercare generated a potential five million contacts. It was vital that its aftercare programmes were perceived well by the customer.

This pattern will vary by type of purchase.

- In fast-moving consumer goods, for example, purchasing frequency is much higher; aftercare would play a minor role in customer satisfaction, while convenience, quality of checkout service, price, choice, parking, and opening hours would be more crucial.
- In the marketing of complex business-to-business products and services, the quality of advice and guidance, the level of pre-sales and after-sales support, and the contribution of other key long-term customer services are crucial factors which determine how well customers are satisfied.

Customer satisfaction guides

The customer satisfaction index, by itself, has little value. It gives an indication of how customers rate local performance and provides a method of comparison, but unless local outlets take action to build on their strengths or improve their weaknesses the questionnaire will be wasted. When a local outlet is participating in a customer satisfaction programme, it should be given a programme guide outlining the reasons for the programme, the business benefits, and the actions the local outlet must take as a result of the programme.

Ford's customer satisfaction programme guide is a comprehensive publication aimed at the dealer principal and the dealership management team. It covers:

- the importance of customer satisfaction;
- the scope of the programme;
- the survey that is the basis of the programme;
- the reasons for the questions;
- the method of calculating the index;
- the management actions that should be taken in response to the questionnaire;
- a department-by-department guide to key customer concerns that have already been identified;
- a summary of actions that other dealers have taken to meet those concerns;
- a development programme for the dealership;
- the training and business programmes available to improve customer satisfaction performance.

The most important sections are the management actions and the departmental guides. A customer satisfaction index is simply a starting point for building a business that is focused on the customer. The programme manual recommends a series of meetings:

- a fortnightly review of all the responses received from customers during the previous period – all questionnaires are returned to a handling agency, which analyses the responses and forwards results and requests for action to individual dealerships once a fortnight;

- a monthly review of action taken in response to the questionnaire;
- a quarterly review of improvements in individual areas and in overall customer satisfaction.

At the fortnightly meetings, departmental managers are given the results of the previous questionnaire and asked to respond to any immediate requests from customers or to deal with any serious complaints within the questionnaires. If, for example, a customer is dissatisfied with a 36,000 mile service, the service manager will be told to contact the customer immediately to find out more information and make a prompt response.

The monthly meetings should focus on more general concerns. If, for example, a large number of customers say they are dissatisfied with parking arrangements or length of time spent in customer reception, the dealership can take action to improve the situation.

The quarterly meeting is a more formal review of progress in improvements and trends in customer satisfaction performance. The dealer principal should take the opportunity to review current improvement projects and to assess whether earlier improvement programmes have had a direct effect on overall customer satisfaction performance levels.

The departmental guides within the customer satisfaction manual are intended to give individual departments a clearer indication of their contribution to customer satisfaction and outline the actions they can take to improve performance. In a questionnaire on standards of service, for example, customers commented on grease marks on their car, cigarettes in the ashtray, radios tuned to a different frequency, or a fault recurring despite the service.

These comments, taken from actual questionnaires, demonstrated to members of staff who don't normally meet customers that there are good reasons for concentrating on customer care, and they show that the department's contribution is important. The section also includes practical examples of what other dealers have done to improve performance in this area. This helps dealers to put together their own action plans.

The customer satisfaction performance guide can be a valuable method of implementing customer care programmes within a local outlet, but it must be an action-oriented programme which local managers can put into immediate use.

Customer satisfaction incentive schemes

The other value of a customer satisfaction index is that it can be used to encourage improvement using recognition and incentive programmes. By providing a quantitive basis for comparison, outlets around the country can compete with each other to demonstrate that they offer the highest levels of satisfaction. This competitive element can be used in a number of ways:

- to incentivise local outlets to improve their own performance on a year-on-year basis;
- to incentivise individual outlets to improve their own performance;
- to encourage the highest standards of customer satisfaction.

The incentive programmes should be based not just on current performance but on improvement, and it must continue to recognise improvement over a long period of time. An extreme version of the incentive programme links local customer satisfaction performance to levels of investment – if an outlet does not achieve targets for customer satisfaction it may not qualify for investment or it may have its own operations restricted. Most programmes however recognise improvement and they can be based on regional or national groupings.

Top-performing outlets in a league receive an award or a prize. A higher status of award can be given to the outlets that achieve the very highest levels of customer satisfaction. A number of programmes operating under the banner of chairman's or president's award recognise excellence in customer satisfaction with a special award for an elite group of branches. Ford's Chairman's Award is an elite pan-European award given to the top dealers in each of 16 territories; they are taken to a top European destination where they are personally recognised by the chairman of Ford of Europe.

Programmes like this help to maintain the impetus of customer care programmes; they ensure that individual departments and outlets aim at continually improving standards.

SUMMARY

This chapter shows how high standards of customer care are essential to building customer satisfaction and loyalty at local level and looks at the different ways in which customer care can be delivered. Customer focus panels, for example, help suppliers and local outlets identify their customers' expectations and the chapter shows how these expectations can be used to develop customer focus standards which can contribute to consistent standards of customer care in every local outlet. The chapter describes a number of different customer care programmes and customer care training options. It also shows the importance of measuring customer satisfaction through customer surveys and how customer comments can be used to compile customer satisfaction guides. Finally, the chapter shows how incentive and recognition schemes can be used to motivate local staff to achieve increasingly higher standards of customer satisfaction.

ACTION CHECKLIST

CUSTOMER CARE

Does your company have a clearly defined customer care policy?

How do your customers rate your customer care performance?

Do you have a clear process for dealing with complaints or queries?

Could you utilise local customer focus panels to raise awareness of customer expectations within your network?

What are the important factors you would seek customers' views on?

Do customer focus standards vary by territory?

Do you have a set of defined customer focus standards?

What impact would customer focus standards have on your business?

CUSTOMER CARE PROGRAMMES

Do you operate customer care programmes?

Do they have measurable results?

What aspects of customer care are most important and could you develop programmes to improve performance?

Can you identify the local staff whose customer care performance is critical to overall success?

Do you provide training for these key staff and can you measure their performance?

Do all your training programmes reflect customer care?

Are your local management teams aware of the importance of customer care and do they encourage their staff to improve their standards?

CUSTOMER SATISFACTION

Do you have formal procedures for measuring customer satisfaction?

Are there common elements of customer satisfaction that work across international markets?

Do your measures allow you to compare outlets across the network and departments within individual outlets?

Do you set progressive customer satisfaction targets and reward improvement?

How often do you measure customer satisfaction and how often do you provide reports to your local outlets?

Is there a procedure for acting on customer satisfaction ratings?

Are your surveys measuring the right factors and are some factors more important than others?

Do you help local outlets to improve their customer satisfaction performance with training and recognition schemes?

Can you tie customer satisfaction ratings to other performance factors to exert greater control over local performance?

Is customer satisfaction treated as a priority in all your territories?

10

IMPROVING SALES PERFORMANCE

INTRODUCTION

A sales development programme is an essential aspect of effective local marketing; by helping local outlets to build sales and relationships with their customers, head-office staff can control and develop long-term turnover and profit. A company can support its local sales effort in a number of ways:

- launching products and services effectively to local outlets and their customers;
- developing sales skills;
- providing product and marketing guides to the complete product range;
- operating structured sales incentives and motivation programmes;
- developing structured customer incentive programmes to encourage repeat business.

These actions will help to build a professional sales operation with minimal use of central resources.

LAUNCHING PRODUCTS AND SERVICES

The first stage in building sales of a new product through a local outlet is to launch the product effectively. Local outlets need to be convinced that the product will help to benefit their business and they need to understand the product or service so that they can market it professionally. The product launch progresses through a number of important stages:

- pre-launch activity to secure distribution and ensure that local outlets have the skills, resources and knowledge to market the product;
- launch events at national, regional or local level;
- launch support to help local outlets make the most of the event.

Pre-launch activity

Pre-launch activity is important to ensure that everything is in place for an effective launch. A launch guide will give the local outlet a list of all the key activities that should be carried out. This is an example of the launch of a fictitious range of business computers through an electrical retailer that traditionally handles only domestic products.

The first section covers the background to the launch and the market opportunities.

- Why is the new product being launched?
- How does it fit into the company's overall strategy?
- What sort of people will buy the product?
- How do they differ from traditional customers?
- What new opportunities does this give the local outlet?
- How are competitors marketing this product?

This section gives local staff an explanation of why the new product is being introduced and demonstrates how it will form an integral part of the group's future development strategy. This is particularly important when the products differ considerably from the current range.

The second part of the guide should explain the features and benefits of the product. It will act as a sales guide for the local outlet staff and will ensure that they fully understand the product. In this example, business computers are likely to need more detailed explanation because the products are unfamiliar. A simple launch guide is unlikely to provide all the knowledge a local salesforce needs, so the guide should also include information on the training and product support available. The guide may even recommend the appointment of a specialist sales executive with the product and marketing knowledge to sell the product at the right level. If training is to be an integral part of the launch programme, the guide will outline the key stages and identify the people who should be involved in the training programme, together with a training schedule.

The third part of the guide should indicate the level of support available for the launch; this will include the launch event itself, the national advertising and promotional programme, together with local marketing programmes. Advance notice allows local outlets to order support material and plan their own local marketing programme so that it is fully integrated with the national launch.

The final part of the guide should provide a schedule and list of key launch activities so that the management team can meet all the requirements of the launch programme. These launch activities might include:

- stock and ordering details;
- training schedule;
- launch events;
- dates for national and local advertising;
- suggested dates and formats for customer events;
- schedule for launch marketing activities.

By specifying and detailing a complete local programme, head-office staff can control the quality and consistency of the local launch and ensure that local and national activities are fully integrated. The pre-launch activity can be managed through a launch guide, but it may be better communicated through direct contact. If the field salesforce is used to present the new programme, it must be trained to discuss it at the right management level. An important event like a product launch must be presented to the complete management team. The salesforce also needs the right level of support material so that it can fully explain the programme.

Launch

With so much pre-launch activity, the main launch event may seem an anti-climax, but a successful event can provide the springboard to rapid national take-up. Chapter 11, 'Developing a contact strategy', describes how products can be launched at regional and local events if there are time and budget constraints, but the national launch remains the emotional high point of any new product programme.

When JCB, the construction equipment manufacturer, launched a new range of versatile diggers, it hired a major exhibition hall and developed a kind of industrial ballet which showed how a group of three diggers could demonstrate complete manoeuvrability. Although this level of creativity may seem unnecessary, it can help to create an emotional atmosphere which generates excitement and attention and is in sharp contrast to the more prosaic marketing presentations that surround it.

New car launches have set the standards for launch events with each manufacturer trying to outdo the others in terms of prestige and innovation. Cars emerging from the floor or bursting through a wall appear to be the norm, while one manufacturer took the opposite approach and moved the entire audience towards the car.

Special effects and theatrical events can certainly add impact to a launch, but location may also be an important determining factor. When a major information technology company wanted to launch a strategically important range of products to its distributors, it chose a location in Europe that was widely regarded as a centre of cultural significance. The launch theme was related to the city's historical background and the delegates were given a prestige launch pack to explain the importance of the programme. The creative theme was continued after the launch event with follow-up direct mail to notify distributors of marketing support and new market opportunities.

Post-launch activity

If the national launch event is the emotional high point of a launch programme, the period after the launch is the critical time for the success of the programme; it is easy to forget the emotion of the special effects, but the real sales effort begins then. The local outlets have to convince their customers that the launch is a significant event.

When Pitman Publishing launched a new book series developed in conjunction with the Institute of Management, it backed it with what was regarded as the largest business book promotion ever put together by one publisher. As well as the general marketing programme which included a large-scale mailing to target readers and a generic advertising campaign in management publications, Pitman Publishing took the opportunity to run a series of local events in conjunction with bookshops. Two hundred bookshops put on special window displays, while seventeen bookshops ran launch events in conjunction with the local branch of the Institute of Management. At each of these events, one of the series authors made a brief presentation to an invited audience of Institute members while members of the Pitman Publishing sales and marketing team helped to arrange hospitality for the evening. This level of support enabled the bookshops to put on a local launch event on a larger scale than would have been possible using their own resources and it enabled Pitman Publishing to ensure a strong presence throughout the country.

PRODUCT AND MARKETING GUIDES

Providing the local salesforce with comprehensive product and market information can help to improve local sales performance by ensuring the salesforce can provide the right level of sales professionalism to its customers.

Keeping product information up to date

The more complex the product or service, the more difficult this becomes. The problem is even more acute when products and legislation change rapidly, as it does in the financial services market, for example.

Insurance companies that use local agents, brokers or independent financial advisers to market their products need to ensure that their representatives are fully up to date with complex products and can provide their customers with a rapid, efficient and professional service. They utilise the increasing power and flexibility of laptop computers to provide the right level of support. The latest generation of laptop computers have the capacity and the processing power to retain information on a wide range of products and services, and to quickly provide customers with personal illustrations or quotes based on specific products. The computers are programmed to lead the representative and the customer step-by-step through all the questions needed to prepare an effective quote and to offer a range of other solutions for comparison. The computer quickly calculates a number of different proposals and provides an instant written quotation. The speed and the professionalism can give the representative an extra edge in a competitive negotiation. From the insurance company's point of view, it can be certain that each transaction is carried out to the same high standards.

The same equipment can be used to carry out sales training; the program can be used to guide a sales representative step-by-step through the process of analysing a customer's needs and developing the right product to meet those needs. To keep the information completely up to date, the database can be easily updated by plugging the laptop computer into a personal computer or corporate network. All the product information can be updated simultaneously, quickly and easily with minimal effort and the insurance company can also be flexible in the way it markets its products. Prices and products can be adjusted on a regional basis to test different marketing strategies.

Technology at the point-of-sale

Technology is also being used at the point-of-sale in retail outlets to improve sales performance. In an electrical retailer, for example, consumers face a bewildering choice of products with features and benefits that look remarkably similar. There are two main problems:

- consumers may not be sure what the real benefits are – an audio system might have 'lots of knobs' but if the majority of those knobs provide no real benefit they might be of little value;
- the consumer may find it difficult to choose between competing models which offer very similar benefits and features or which offer two different sets of benefits.

The problem is compounded by the fact that one store might stock competing products from four or more manufacturers and each manufacturer supply its own product information in a different format. The salesforce has to make up its own mind which is the better product. In a retail environment where the sales staff might be part time or even casual, it is hardly surprising that customers felt they were not getting the best possible advice before buying. This 'pile it high and shift it' attitude might have been effective when price was the only consideration, but with both products and consumers becoming more sophisticated, the need for comprehensive, easy-to-use product information has become more vital.

In this case it was important that the retailer, rather than the manufacturer, controlled the information in order to avoid accusations of bias. The retailer used the capabilities of interactive video to develop a self-selection sales demonstration that would guide sales staff and consumers through the minefield of conflicting features and benefits. Consumers were asked to decide which features they rated as most important; they nominated the price range within their budget and the video then gave them a short list of suitable products. Consumers could either make their own selection or review the products with sales staff.

Giving the customer the choice of freedom from sales pressure is a development that may grow. The Rover Group identified the trend when it opened a 'sales-free zone' in a London showroom. The showroom had a series of interactive videos and information points where customers could get help and advice when they needed it. There was plenty of product literature and free-standing displays, but customers did not have to face the ordeal of interrogation by sales staff. Although the unmanned showroom is unlikely to have a great future, this experiment shows the potential of effective product information at the point-of-sale.

Product manuals

Traditional methods of providing the salesforce with the right level of product and market information will continue to be important. When Securitag, a specialist software company supplying security tags and access control systems, wanted to improve the performance of its international distributor network, it identified product information as the key area for development. The distributors had been handling less-sophisticated products and were not familiar with the technology or the operation of the company's products. Securitag had originally planned to produce a user manual specifically for distributors which explained how to use and program the tags.

The user guide was simplified and expanded to incorporate a complete guide to the product and its application. The distributor staff used the information to identify sales opportunities in their territory and develop a professional product presentation.

When Case Europe, the agricultural and construction equipment manufacturer, wanted to improve customer loyalty and build sales of its parts and service operations, it identified product knowledge as the key to success. The company ran a pan-European advertising campaign to raise customer awareness of its parts and service capability, but it realised that the standard of service available from local branches must match the promise of the advertising which described the professionalism of the service. Case put together a comprehensive product guide linked to a skills training programme and an incentive scheme which recognised parts and service marketing skills.

STRUCTURED INCENTIVE SCHEMES

Incentive schemes are an integral part of a sales management operation; they can be used to motivate sales staff to improve their overall sales performance or they can be structured to improve performance in specific areas such as repeat sales, new accounts or the acquisition of new skills. The Case example demonstrates a number of these principles in action. Case identified that it could build sales and customer loyalty by providing the highest standards of customer care to its service customers. The incentive scheme was carefully structured to improve performance in all the areas critical to achieving that objective. It covered:

- participation in the parts and service training programme;

- new accounts opened;
- percentage of repeat business achieved;
- achievement of fleet parts and service contracts;
- sales of products identified for seasonal promotion.

Distributors were assessed on a series of long- and short-term objectives that would help them build a specific type of business. The same approach can be used to encourage dealers to stock certain types of seasonal products or to focus on sales of a certain product line. The important point about these types of incentive schemes is that they are structured to encourage continuous effort over a period of time, unlike short-term incentives.

Sales incentives have traditionally been geared to moving stock quickly for tactical reasons and, as such, they are an essential sales management technique, but they can also be used in a strategic way.

When a European vehicle paint manufacturer wanted to build a broader customer base, rather than depend on a few large customers, it developed a year-long incentive programme for its distributors. It wanted to encourage distributors to win and retain business from independent bodyshops as well as the franchised car dealers that represented only a small part of the market. Points were awarded for opening new accounts with the independents and a structured bonus system applied to percentage increases in business with these new accounts. The distributors were also given points for increasing business with existing accounts, but these were weighted to count for less in the overall assessment.

The company also wanted to encourage distributors to acquire new skills in business development so that they could form closer working relationships with their customers at senior management level. Additional points were awarded for participation in business skills training courses and for achieving different training levels. Finally, the incentive programme awarded points for participation in a number of business-development programmes which would enable the distributor to improve the quality of service to customers. The incentive programme encouraged overall business development rather than short-term tactical sales.

To maintain interest in the programme, the manufacturer offered different levels of prizes. There were regular monthly prizes for best sales performance with quarterly regional awards for best overall performance. The regional winners were then allowed to go forward to a European incentive programme which rewarded the high achievers with more attractive prizes. The programme had depth as well as breadth.

CUSTOMER INCENTIVE PROGRAMMES

Incentive programmes can also be used to encourage customers to buy from the same local outlet. While petrol stations and food retailers have now got the technique down to a fine art, the same techniques are now being adapted by a more conservative audience.

A proposal to a high-street bank suggested that structured incentive schemes could be used to increase car loan business in branches around the country. Bank customers tend to move their current accounts infrequently, if ever, so the bank has an opportunity to build higher levels of repeat business over the customer's lifetime. Bank customers are also likely to change their cars as their personal circumstances change. It would therefore be profitable for the bank to offer a long-term structured programme to retain its car loan business.

The incentive programme was structured as a bank car club with members being entitled to special offers on motoring-related products and services from a choice of national and local suppliers. The programme therefore had the flexibility to be tailored to local conditions by allowing branches to make their own arrangements with local motoring organisations. Because motoring was regarded as a specialist activity, branches were encouraged to appoint someone with motoring interests as the car loan specialist. To add further interest, staff within each branch were invited to participate in a special incentive programme related to loan enquiries and loans completed on car purchases.

The long-term potential of the programme allowed the bank to offer future discounts on the purchase of replacement vehicles or additional family cars. The customer was offered a choice of short-

and long-term incentives to arrange other car loans with the bank and the scheme offered branches a great deal of local flexibility.

When ICL wanted to encourage its customers to purchase more professional services to support their information systems, it introduced a programme called ProSelect, which offered customers long-term discounts on their purchases. The branch customer-service manager worked with the customer to identify the likely service requirement over the next year and to develop a schedule for service delivery. The service manager then calculated the total cost and allocated the costs over a twelve-month period. If the customer chose ProSelect, he or she could determine the timing of the service delivery, but payments were smoothed over a twelve-month period. This meant that a customer could take on a large project at the beginning of the year and pay for it later. This helped customers plan and fund their work more efficiently, and it also helped the branch to develop closer working relationships and gain a better understanding of its customers' service needs.

SUMMARY

This chapter looks at a number of ways of helping local outlets to build sales and improve relationships with their customers. It begins by looking at the critical area of launching new products and services, showing how comprehensive information and support at each stage of the launch can help to build understanding, commitment and a successful launch. The same principles can be applied to existing products and services and the chapter looks at different approaches to providing product and marketing information. It shows how to keep information up to date using new technology such as laptop computers and interactive video and explains how these tools can be used to improve the selling process to the customer. The chapter gives examples of different types of incentive programme and shows how they can be structured to meet different marketing objectives.

ACTION CHECKLIST

NEW PRODUCTS

How important are new products to the success of your business?

What are the key stages in the launch of your new products?

Do your local outlets have the skills and resources to launch the product effectively?

Are there high-risk areas where you may need to take action to ensure a successful launch?

How will you present the new product to your local outlets?

Will the presentation have sufficient impact to motivate them to succeed?

Is the support you are providing sufficient to ensure success?

How do you intend to maintain the momentum of the launch after the initial presentations?

How will you measure the success of the launch?

Are you entering new international markets where all your products are new products?

Do you have to raise customer awareness of your products in international markets?

PRODUCT INFORMATION

Are you marketing complex products where a high level of product knowledge is needed?

Do you have to raise salesforce awareness of your products in international markets?

Do customers expect sales staff to demonstrate good product knowledge?

Does product information change rapidly?

Do your sales guides reflect market differences in international markets?

Can you use new technology to communicate product information to the local salesforce and to customers?

How important is product demonstration, and could it be handled more effectively?

INCENTIVE PROGRAMMES

Are your sales incentive programmes structured to reflect short- and long-term marketing objectives?

Can you include factors such as training, product knowledge, customer retention and new business development in your incentive programmes?

Do you use incentives to achieve short-term tactical gains or do you build them over a period of time?

Can you identify a means of incentivising customers to continue purchasing over a period of time?

Are customer incentives important in establishing market share in new international markets?

11

DEVELOPING A CONTACT STRATEGY

INTRODUCTION

To make a network operate effectively, it is essential to maintain contact with local outlets. How many times has the local office accused head office of being remote and out of touch? Can head-office staff be certain that local outlets are aware of the latest product information or the current operating policy? Is there a feeling that certain outlets are better informed or supported than others?

Formal and informal information channels are used to maintain effective contact with local staff at all levels and, as part of the planning process, you should be concerned with developing a contact strategy to meet the following objectives:

- local managers understand your current business objectives;
- managers understand their responsibilities and objectives;
- managers understand corporate operating procedures;
- managers are aware of the business and marketing support available to their outlet;
- managers are committed to success;
- staff understand the relationship between the local outlet and head office;
- staff have up-to-date product knowledge and understand how to implement company policies;
- staff feel that they have a worthwhile career structure within the organisation.

Within those overall objectives, there may be more specific objectives that are relevant to your network, but the main principles are:

- keep local staff and management fully informed;
- use communications to motivate them to succeed.

USING COMMUNICATIONS TO MOTIVATE

A company that managed fleet petrol costs through a company charge card operated an incentive programme for petrol retailers to sign up more card holders in their local market. Although the company dealt with major fleets at a corporate level, it was keen to build business with smaller local fleets using the retailers as a gateway. The company magazine published a regular report on the prizes awarded to successful retailers that had signed up most new customers. Yet, when the manager of one of the country's most successful retailers was approached for comments on the programme, he claimed that he was not aware his outlet had won a prize; he said that he was never told whether any of the application forms he returned had been converted to live accounts, and he found the whole scheme to be a 'nuisance'.

Clearly, this manager was not motivated to succeed, even though he was running one of the most successful outlets in the network. How much more successful would the incentive programme have been if the card operator had issued the following communications:

- sent a personal letter congratulating the winners;
- issued a management report to each outlet listing the converted applications;
- issued an analysis of the business generated from each outlet's cards.

This would have ensured that the manager perceived a return for his efforts in marketing the card to potential customers – a return in both personal and business terms.

USING COMMUNICATIONS TO IMPROVE SERVICE

The Joint Credit Card Company (JCC), which issued and managed the Access brand credit card on behalf of a number of high-street banks, recognised the importance of communicating with staff at all levels. It understood that the checkout was a critical element in the relationship between card issuer and card holder. If customers experienced difficulty or delay in having a credit card transaction processed, they would have a poor perception of the card issuer. JCC also understood that the people who carried out the initial processing of the credit card payments were often casual staff who were unlikely to have had any formal training in credit card processing. JCC published a regular magazine called 'Tilltalk' which was distributed to all retailers accepting the Access credit card. 'Tilltalk' contained easy-to-understand features on the different types of credit card available, tips on processing and checking card details, information on credit card legislation and regular features on fraud. The magazine also ran regular competitions for checkout staff which offered good prizes and were based on product knowledge and processing skills.

Because the format was easy to understand, checkout staff read the magazine and improved the quality of their service. Training departments in large retail groups used the magazine as the basis for their training programmes. JCC was therefore able to improve standards of credit card processing at local level without investing in a major local training infrastructure. It also gained the loyalty of checkout staff who were often regarded as an under-skilled casual labour force. It was able to offer local outlets what was effectively free training for their own staff. Regular communications like this influenced both staff and management attitudes in a positive way.

THE IMPORTANCE OF PERSONAL CONTACT

Personal contact is also important in domestic and international markets. RHP Bearings, an international precision engineering group, sold bearings to most of the industrial countries in the world. In the major industrialised markets such as the USA, Germany, Italy, France and South Africa, it set up a local marketing subsidiary which had local participation, equity and management. However, in emerging territories, it relied on agents and distributors to sell its products and establish its reputation. Although the distributors, in the main, were engineering specialists, they did not have the in-depth knowledge of the product or the market to service the most demanding customers. Paper-based communications would have given them a sound background in the bearing business, but often this was not sufficient. There were also opportunities to make high-level presentations to potentially important customers, but the distributors felt they did not have the experience to take full advantage.

RHP's solution was to appoint resident managers in key growth territories whose task was to work with distributors to develop local business. The most important aspect of this solution was that the RHP people were in the territory and not making flying visits from head office on firefighting missions. The resident managers were able to maintain regular contact with the local distributors to provide them with the level of support and expertise needed to succeed and to deal with any queries promptly and efficiently.

The resident managers were able to get a better feel for local market conditions and provide a level of support that was relevant to the market. Most importantly, RHP was able to build up a high level of personal contact with local distributors which removed any concern about having to implement remote head-office programmes. The effect was described by the current chairman as 'our personal presence in the local market'.

This strategy proved to be an important element in RHP's international growth although perhaps the example of the resident manager appointed to Iran shortly before the revolution proves the point that you can never be too aware of local market conditions.

Personal contact and published communications are just two elements of a comprehensive contact strategy. The remainder of this chapter will consider the ways in which different types of communication can be used to achieve the objectives; they include:

- national conferences;
- regional business meetings;
- individual briefings;
- visit programmes;
- appointment of distributor specialist;

- staff communications;
- magazines;
- distributor business, marketing and technical bulletins.

Each of these elements has a role to play in improving communications between head office and the local outlet. The first three elements – individual briefings, regional business meetings and national conferences – are used to bring local branches up to date with significant developments that affect their business such as a new product launch or a change in company policy.

NATIONAL CONFERENCES

The high point of any local contact strategy is the national conference which representatives from every outlet are invited to attend, and where the event may last for a longer period of time than a normal meeting. The conference is usually held for a major event such as the launch of a new product or a presentation of annual results and is designed to generate high levels of enthusiasm and commitment. A national conference has the additional benefit of bringing together people from around the local network who would not normally meet each other, so it has a considerable team building value.

Building team spirit

ICL, the European information systems group, had held a traditional national conference for its management team from all its divisions, but individual divisions held only small, simple meetings where it was convenient. When the Customer Service division was reorganised to reflect its changing importance within the group, the divisional marketing team took the opportunity to give the change a higher profile. As part of the national three-day conference, the division organised its own 'kick-off' event - a mini-conference – using all the resources of the main conference. Because key group managers were already in attendance at the main conference, the divisional conference was able to attract high-level speakers and provide a broader perspective to the delegates.

The divisional conference was able to use the conference projection and production facilities to make a high standard of presentation to delegates. Video and multi-screen slide presentations were unheard of at previous divisional events. The presentation format gave a clear signal to the delegates that the division meant business and, more importantly, it raised the profile of the division within the group, helping to build understanding and awareness of its new role.

The point about any national conference is that it should have purpose and it should be handled effectively. Many product launches have a high theatrical content – Chapter 10, 'Improving sales performance', describes this in more detail – because the intention is to create impact. Car manufacturers, for example, take their dealers to exotic locations when they launch a new model. The high point of the event is the launch itself which demands great impact, but the remainder of the time can be spent in building the right level of team spirit among distributors.

With the increasing emphasis on global branding and global marketing, company conferences are frequently held on an international scale. An international conference not only brings together staff who are separated by physical barriers, it also helps to raise awareness of the scale of global expertise and help to build consistent standards and performance. IBM was once rumoured to have brought together communications and documentation specialists from all over the world for a convention to agree standard names and descriptions for all its products. The value of an international conference might be reduced if the local companies operate separate product and marketing programmes, but they are essential if the company is pursuing a global marketing strategy.

Rewarding effort

The national conference can also be used as a reward for high achievement. Ford Motor Company runs a number of annual incentive and recognition programmes for dealership staff at different levels. Although the intention is to encourage the staff to achieve higher levels of performance or increase sales, the events also help to encourage a sense of belonging to the organisation. The

Chairman's Award for Customer Satisfaction was an exclusive programme for dealership heads throughout Europe. The award was
given only to a small number of dealerships that had achieved
extremely high standards of customer care and the event was held in a
European location that reflected the inspirational standards of the
programme. The highlight of the programme was the individual
presentation to the winning dealership by the Chairman of Ford of
Europe, an event that represented real status to the dealership. The
high profile of the programme raised its importance among the whole
dealer body and encouraged high levels of participation and effort.

The Parts Merit Club was aimed at Ford dealer parts sales
managers and was awarded for sales success and performance in a
number of crucial parts marketing programmes. The Merit Club
rapidly achieved cult status among parts sales managers and it
became one of the most fiercely contested incentive events in the
Ford calendar. Many parts sales managers confessed that they put in
extra effort to achieve their Merit Club targets so that they could
attend the annual convention – the programme had the desired effect
of building business and building teamwork.

REGIONAL BUSINESS MEETINGS

National and international conferences have an important role to
play in building team spirit and raising awareness of new developments, but they can be expensive and time consuming. Unless the
event is extremely important to business development, it may be
more satisfactory to consider regional business meetings. Busy
managers appreciate the fact that they need commit only part of a
working day to the event and they can cut down unnecessary travelling time. Given the current climate for reducing headcount and
making the most of existing teams, this could be an important consideration. Regional business meetings are a valuable format for
maintaining personal contact – they allow national groupings of local
outlets – and they enable a supplier to hold a concentrated meeting to
bring local outlets up to date with key events.

Although regional meetings do not have the high profile of national conferences, they represent an opportunity to maintain regular contact at a high level. The events should include presentations by senior management from the head-office team and should concentrate on national policy as well as matters of regional interest. Motor manufacturers adopt a half-day format for their regional business meetings. Delegates arrive at mid-day for an informal lunch before a series of afternoon briefings covering new products, company developments, management changes, promotional activities, pricing, marketing programmes and objectives for the next quarter. The meetings give the head-office team an opportunity to update local outlets on current activities and maintain contact between the management teams. These events are held quarterly and the meeting dates provide a focal point for product announcements or the launch of other developments.

PRODUCT ANNOUNCEMENTS

Many information systems companies have a formal programme of announcement dates which provide a useful basis for operating regional business meetings. These announcement dates are not necessarily major product launches, but they may include the introduction of a new version of an existing product or the launch of a minor product within an existing range. The information-systems companies are able to utilise the announcement programmes to focus the attention of their dealers and their local branches on business and marketing objectives.

BRANCH BRIEFINGS

While the regional business meetings provide a convenient practical alternative to national conferences for frequently-held events that do not need a high-profile environment, they still have drawbacks. If a supplier wants to brief an entire local management team or other members of the staff, or if the briefing is confidential to one particular outlet, regular meetings may prove impractical.

When European vehicle refinisher Spies Hecker launched its product range into the UK, it introduced new marketing techniques and demanded new sales skills from the UK marketing team. A key element of their marketing strategy was the 'Partners in Profit' programme which enabled the manufacturer and distributors to work together to build distributors' business. The manufacturer provided a programme of business and marketing support together with business systems to facilitate improvements in sales and profitability. To launch the programme to distributors, it was important to involve a number of different members of the distributor management team: the directors, bodyshop manager, parts manager, service manager and business manager. The programme was also confidential to a degree because it included levels of support tailored to individual outlets and included information that would not readily be supplied to competitive distributors.

The ideal solution was a presentation tailored to individual branch needs and given on the branch premises. The supplier was able to get together the whole distributor team in a location that was convenient and did not take up much of the team's valuable time. Spies Hecker was also able to make contact with members of the distributor team who would not normally be in touch with the salesforce. By putting together its own presentation team for the event, it was able to provide the right level of skills and seniority.

The branch briefing provides a valuable method of contact for the supplier, however it should not be treated as just another business meeting. Wherever possible, the meeting should be treated as a special event with a dedicated meeting room and professional presentation techniques. Informal contact at the local outlet is an essential part of the process and is described in detail later in the chapter. The branch briefing should have a more formal structure and should resemble the main conference presentation in all but location.

APPOINTING A DISTRIBUTOR SPECIALIST

Day-to-day contact with local outlets is a specialist activity which needs to be managed properly and not treated as an ad-hoc activity.

Many companies appoint a branch or distributor specialist to take responsibility for this aspect of business development. The distributor specialist would carry out a wide range of tasks including:

- maintain research of all business activities;
- provide a support service;
- deal with local enquiries;
- process orders and maintain progress on local business;
- maintain regular contact and ensure that local outlets are kept up to date with important information about the supplier;
- advise local outlets on company policy;
- gain an understanding of the local outlet's business;
- help the local outlet develop business and marketing plans.

The distributor specialist is a key point of contact for all local outlets and should be perceived as a partner.

Ford, for example, recommended that its dealers appoint a fleet parts specialist to deal directly with local fleet managers and provide high levels of support to fleet customers. The specialist is not just a member of the sales team; he or she has to take part in a training programme to develop the right level of professional skills to deliver a quality service. It is important that local contact is delivered professionally and planned carefully to optimise the benefits. As well as developing the right skills through training, the fleet parts specialist is responsible for operating a comprehensive visit programme to introduce new products and procedures and ensure that local outlets are implementing fleet business programmes effectively. For example, when new marketing programmes are introduced, the specialist works closely with local outlets to explain the programmes and provide initial advice and guidance on operating them. This ensures that the local branches operate the programmes effectively.

Although Ford was using the fleet specialist to support its distributors, the same principle can be applied to a local branch/head-office relationship. A management consultancy operates a network of local branches to provide customers with a local service. It operates a central group marketing service, but also appoints a series of regional marketing offices staffed by specialists who are able to offer a customised local support service to its branches.

N&P Building Society appoints local marketing and public relations specialists to support its national and local marketing policies. The marketing specialists operate within the guidelines of group policy, but because they are familiar with the local market, they are able to provide a highly responsive service that is geared to local market conditions. This is a policy that clearly recognises the importance of customised local marketing.

STAFF COMMUNICATIONS PROGRAMMES

Contact programmes are not just important for ensuring high levels of performance, they can help to motivate staff and ensure that they are committed to success. Contact programmes ensure that staff are fully aware of everything that is happening within a company and understand the reasons for any changes.

Explaining change

When ICL changed the way it delivered service to its regional customers, it ran an internal communications programme aimed at explaining the nature of the change to local branch staff. The ICL customer base was originally segmented by region with branch offices in different parts of the country. Each branch regarded its customers as its own and it employed service staff who dealt with these customers. ICL wanted to make the most effective use of its national and international service resources so that they could deliver a consistent quality service to their customers, wherever they were located. Under the original system, the branch could deliver only the quality of service matched by its resources, and customers in more remote regions tended to get a reduced service.

ICL introduced a central service contact point for all customers – the Customer Reception Centre – which drew on the resources of a number of centres of excellence to provide the right response to the customer. Service engineers were still based at the branches, but contact had been removed from the branches. To ensure that branch staff did not feel demotivated, ICL put together a presentation and a programme of communications to explain the changes and keep branch staff up to date with the progress of the project. The communications explained the changing role of the branch and showed how it could contribute to customer satisfaction.

By demonstrating that local branches played a positive role and by keeping them fully informed on all aspects of the programme, ICL was able to build commitment and motivation. The alternative to informed commitment is ignorance and gossip which can be destructive and can damage customer relations as well as the quality of service.

Using new communications technology

While personal contact remains the strongest form of communications between head office and local outlets, high levels of contact may not be possible because of resource problems. A local contact strategy should include a comprehensive programme of communications to keep staff up to date. The traditional method of communications has been to issue published material such as magazines, newspapers or staff bulletins; however, with the growing sophistication of video technology and the development of private broadcast networks, many international companies are installing video links in all their offices to broadcast the equivalent of a corporate television programme.

STC, for example, set up a system of video monitors in the reception areas of all its main offices. Visitors and staff were able to get a brief news round-up of developments within the company which was updated daily. The programme included:

- financial and share information;
- brief presentations on new product development;
- interviews with key personnel on important developments within the group;
- the group's views on current economic and business activities.

There was also an additional module of material for STC group staff only which covered news of appointments within the group, developments affecting staff and personal news that might be of interest to colleagues. The group was therefore able to maintain high-quality communications presented in a professional manner, and keep employees fully informed on all aspects of the company's activities.

Companies in the motor industry are utilising video and cable technology to provide dealers with an integrated communications service. They provide the news service on new company developments and broadcast details of national and regional advertising campaigns and other promotions. They can also target dealers with specific information on local marketing activities. The same video networks can be used to broadcast training programmes for different members of staff, reducing the overall cost of training and making training more convenient and accessible.

While such sophisticated video links may be outside the scope of most companies, an increasing number of organisations have computer links with their local networks. These links can be used to issue urgent information at very short notice. Given the quality of graphics now available on many personal computer systems, it would be possible to issue regular business bulletins with full supporting charts and graphics and to present brief summaries for financial or business performance. By using emerging computer technology, it is also possible to produce highly illustrated product and corporate slide presentations which can be integrated with a contact strategy.

Printed communications

However, most companies will rely on traditional printed material for their communications. Company newspapers and magazines, for example, can be produced at reasonable cost for distribution to all local staff. They contain a mixture of business and personal news designed to keep local staff fully informed of company developments and build team spirit.

The German chemicals group, Hoechst, produces a range of staff magazines for local offices:

• a management bulletin issued to managers throughout all European locations provides a regular briefing on key issues and developments within the group;

- an employee magazine mixes European business development with personal and social information published on a country-by-country basis;
- operating companies within specialist divisions and their distributors also receive an industry-specific newspaper or magazine, which focuses on technical developments as well as corporate information.

The group therefore achieves an important balance between national, international, group and industry-specific information.

Powertalk International, published by Ford's GRI power products division, is issued to power products dealers throughout the world. The magazine, compiled by a professional editor, includes features from customers around the world and is translated into seven languages. The magazine is recognised as an authoritative source of information on the power products business and its contents are frequently used as training material by dealers. The magazine is an important element of GRI's distributor contact strategy for a number of reasons:

- dealers are actively involved in seeking out application stories and setting up interviews for the editor – they feel that it is their magazine;
- copies of the magazine are also sent to important customers, providing a useful form of customer relations for the distributors;
- countries and distributors compete with each other to get their material into the magazine, increasing the appeal and value of the magazine;
- the magazine provides a valuable form of product and application training apart from its intrinsic public relations value.

This double-edged role improves the quality of contact and ensures that the communications work hard. An accountancy group that operates regional and international branches issued an internal magazine that acted as a source of information on changes in legislation. The magazine contained a series of feature articles written by consultants on current issues. They helped local branches to identify business opportunities and also ensured that local staff were able to draw on the skills and expertise of head-office staff who were effectively acting as a centre of excellence.

SUMMARY

This chapter discusses the crucial role of communications in improving local marketing performance. It outlines important objectives for a communications programme that will build understanding and commitment to success. The chapter shows how communications can be used to motivate local staff by recognising achievement and provides an example of the way effective communications can help to improve standards of customer service. The chapter reinforces the importance of personal contact in national and international markets and shows how national conferences, regional business meetings and branch briefings provide contact options to meet different communications objectives. The chapter recommends the appointment of a distributor specialist to concentrate on the quality of communications with local outlets, and outlines the specialist's key responsibilities. Finally, the chapter describes a number of options for improving staff communications using advanced technology such as corporate television networks or traditional printed material.

ACTION CHECKLIST

IMPORTANCE OF COMMUNICATIONS

Do you have a clear communications strategy?

Who are the most important contacts in the local outlets?

What do they need to know to carry out their responsibilities effectively?

Do you need to improve motivation or understanding within your local outlets?

If you are entering new international markets, what is the current understanding of your organisation and your products?

Do customer surveys suggest that there is a lack of understanding of certain key issues within the local outlets?

Can you measure the effectiveness of your local communications?

Can you simplify your communications to ensure comprehension and understanding?

PERSONAL CONTACT

How important is personal contact in your business?

What is the current level of personal contact and how could it be improved?

Is personal contact with local outlets the responsibility of a specialist or is it left to chance?

What opportunities are there to improve the level and quality of customer contact?

Are you taking full advantage of all the meeting opportunities?

Does your meeting programme accommodate the needs of your international network?

Could you increase the number of effective meetings without imposing on management time?

What is the level of team spirit within your network and could it be improved by more frequent contact?

Do your local teams feel they are out of touch with events at the centre of the network?

Do you bring your local teams together to recognise achievement?

Are you maintaining personal contact at the right level within your local outlets?

Could you appoint a specialist to handle local communications, and what would the specialist's responsibilities be?

Could you appoint a resident manager to handle local communications in your international networks?

STAFF COMMUNICATIONS

Are local staff fully up to date with developments within your organisation?

Do you communicate major change effectively throughout the network?

Do your communications encourage participation?

Can you use communications technology to improve the speed or impact of your communications?

12

WORKING IN PARTNERSHIP

INTRODUCTION

A good working relationship is an essential link between supplier and local outlet, but the relationship will improve even more when the two work in partnership. Partnership is rarely a formal contractual agreement, rather it is an attitude in which two parties work together to achieve mutually beneficial objectives. It may be as simple as agreeing to jointly work together to capture one major account or it may involve more formal arrangements in which supplier and local outlet utilise communications technology to share information and resources and improve their joint performance.

Franchised distributor agreements are a form of partnership in which the supplier supports the local outlet's complete business and doesn't just provide marketing support. The independent local outlet rarely has such a close working relationship with the supplier and may simply co-operate in an informal way. Partnership should be mutually beneficial and it should provide each party with access to scarce skills and resources that would otherwise involve considerable investment.

PROVIDING NATIONWIDE RESOURCES

As aftercare service grows in importance, suppliers aim to provide their customers with the higher standards of service throughout the country. They have a number of choices:

- set up their own service network, involving a major investment in service infrastructure and skills;
- use an independent service organisation on a third party basis;
- work in partnership with an independent service organisation to establish a joint service network conforming to the supplier's quality standards.

The first option is feasible when the supplier already has an established service operation and simply has to expand it, but this is an option that can be difficult and the operation would have to be scaled up and down to meet different levels of business.

The second option – working with an independent – appears to be satisfactory in some circumstances, but the network may be unsuitable and the service provider may not be able to operate to the levels of quality that the supplier needs.

The third option, working in partnership with a network of independent service organisations, provides a flexible solution and can benefit both parties.

As an example, take an engineering company with an established network of distributors that employ their own service technicians. In the past, the engineering company has handled service and maintenance directly through a small in-house team and has provided a spare parts service through the distributor network to any customers' with their own service teams. The distributor service staff provided service directly to smaller companis or may have provided emergency cover to customers' with their own in-house teams. However an increasing number of companies are disbanding their own service teams and outsourcing. If the engineering company is to retain contact and not lose control to third-party service organisations, it needs to provide nationwide cover, but it does not have the resources.

The engineering company decide that the distributor service network provides a good basis for the service programme and sets up a partnership agreement with the distributors. The engineering company agrees to support the distributors in the following ways:

- provide full product training for service staff;
- provid full technical support to the service staff;
- provide access to the company's service database;

- develop service tools to enable the distributor service staff to handle more complex service tasks;
- set up simplified ordering procedures so that service staff get the parts they need quickly;
- develop quality standards in conjunction with distributor staff so that the service is delivered to an agreed standard;
- set up a central service reception facility so that customers can easily contact the appropriate service centre to get service anywhere in the country;
- communicate the nationwide service network to their customers.

These actions enable the distributors to improve the performance of their own service operations and to provide the level of service needed by the engineering company. The distributors, for their part, would agree to the following actions:

- participate in the manufacturer's training programme;
- conform to quality standards that were jointly agreed;
- maintain adequate stock levels to provide adequate service cover;
- give priority to the company's service business;
- comply with response levels.

The partnership agreement benefits both parties:

- the engineering company acquires a quality nationwide service network with the minimum investment and is able to provide a high level of service to customers;
- the dealers improve their own service performance and gain access to additional sources of service business.

The same principles of co-operation and support can be applied to training. The recent Training Enterprise Council (TEC) initiative, which seeks to co-ordinate training skills and resources throughout the country and to integrate these with the country's changing training needs, is an example of partnership in operation at a number of different levels:

- the government and the central TEC co-ordinate the nationwide network of regional TECs and set overall objectives;
- the central TEC provides advice and guidance, training, support

and budgets to the regional TECs to ensure that they have the skills and resources to provide a cost-effective professional local service;

- the regional TECs work in partnership with local businesses and education authorities to identify local training requirements and raise awareness of the importance of training within schools, colleges and the business community;
- the regional TECs work in partnership with local training organisations to ensure an effective local network of service providers which provide a comprehensive training service to TEC's customers.

Using the principles of partnership, a complete nationwide training service has been established without any formal business relationships. The final partnership at regional level illustrates the principle most effectively:

- the local service providers run independent training organisations, but they act as service deliverers for the TECs;
- the TECs promote the training service to schools, colleges and businesses and also provide a range of financial assistance to trainees and their employers;
- the service providers benefit from TEC's generic marketing of training and the funding available to boost training budgets;
- the TECS also provide a training management and administration service, using a centralised booking and charging service, thereby relieving the administrative burden on the training organisations;
- the TECs benefit because they can co-ordinate training operations to meet national policies and regional requirements but they do not have to invest in a national training infrastructure.

BROADENING THE SERVICE

A growing trend in the marketing services business has been for networks of individual consultancies to work together to provide an integrated solution to clients' problems. They can draw on each other's skills and resources to put together a complete project team and they can refer business within the group. The principle is known as networking and it can be based on formal or informal relationships.

For example, a marketing services network, which could consist of associates or members of a holding group, might include companies or individuals specialising in research, design, advertising, photography, video, training and event management. Each of the companies would have its own client list, buying specialist services but, for certain large-scale projects, the group could put together a team providing all the different disciplines. This partnership enables each company to build a separate, clearly defined business, but provides the opportunities for additional business and enables the group to develop a competitive quality service across a broad range of disciplines.

In the retail design sector, the same principle of multi-disciplinary networks has emerged. Large retail chains that have redeveloped their operations have used multi-disciplinary teams of architects, interior designers, graphic designers, product development specialists, training specialists and merchandising companies. Sometimes the consortium has been put together from separate companies but in many cases the programme has been handled by loose groupings who operate within a network.

The network approach can also be used to develop international business where groups of professional service companies draw on each other's skills and resources and provide a local service to each other's clients. In the advertising business, the increasing importance of global brands and global marketing strategies means that advertising agencies now have to offer an international network of offices to serve clients in all their key markets. Many of the giants of the industry such as Saatchi and Saatchi, described earlier in the book, have built their global network by acquisition and merger, but others rely on working partnerships to offer their clients an international service.

The Design Network is an international consortium of independent design companies based in all the major European countries. Each company has its own client base, but it handles local client contact for multi-disciplinary clients. The members of the group can also draw on central computer-graphics and design facilities and make effective use of the investment. A partnership approach like this is ideal for professional services companies that wish to broaden their service offering or expand their regional, national or international service.

JOINT VENTURES

Many of the partnerships described in this chapter have worked in favour of the supplier, helping them to extend the reach and scope of their business, but partnership can also be used to grow the local business and enable it to develop a successful small business. Here, the supplier or head-office team work in close conjunction with the local outlet to develop a targeted sales proposal and field a strong team to win a major piece of new business for the local outlet.

Traigon, a company specialising in security packaging for the financial sector and the security market, markets its products in Europe through independent distributors. Its distributors have considerable experience in selling related products to financial institutions, but they do not have depth of knowledge of the Traigon product. When they identified an opportunity to build business with the domestic banks, they approached Traigon to help them develop a joint presentation when they were negotiating with corporate purchasing teams at head-office level. Traigon was able to provide the technical and marketing expertise plus marketing communications support to win the business.

RHP Bearings, part of an international engineering group, worked with a selected group of engineering distributors in the UK to help them win a major parts and service contract with a major public organisation. The distributors had a network of branches located strategically near each of the customer's main depots; they had the product range to meet the customer's demands and their staff were already dealing with the customer on ad-hoc purchases. To make an effective pitch for the business, the distributors needed to strengthen their business in a number of areas:

- scheduled, guaranteed delivery without major stockholding;

- technical support and back-up;
- availability of special products;
- competitive prices on high-volume purchases;
- emergency service to keep the customer operations running.

RHP was able to provide the continuity of supply and the back-up the distributors needed by analysing the customer's scheduled and emergency stock requirements and developing supply schedules that would enable the distributor to provide guaranteed cover in a cost-effective way. The partnership arrangement benefited both parties because RHP was able to increase its business with the distributors without the cost of setting up a supply network to service a large multi-site customer and the distributors were able to build on their existing local relationship with the customer to increase their business and secure a major contract.

STRONGER BUSINESS LINKS

Partnership can help manufacturers and distributors gain additional business by working more closely on special projects, but there are also opportunities to improve overall business performance by building stronger business links. Developments in Electronic Data Interchange and other communications links are helping to speed up and simplify transactions between distributors and manufacturers and enabling them to share business information.

Several years ago, the major breweries introduced computerised cash terminals into public houses, restaurants and other licensed premises. The terminals enabled local managers to improve management at the independent outlet and they also enabled the breweries to control their regional networks more effectively from head office. The terminals recorded all transactions and also automatically adjusted stock levels. The transactions could be itemised by department – public bar, saloon bar, restaurant, discotheque, off-license sales – so that the local manager could analyse the performance of each department and assess the effect of price changes or other marketing activities.

The terminals also provided stock-management and financial information for local action and for central analysis and control. Head office can quickly analyse performance on a daily basis for the entire network and adjust production and marketing activities to suit the current planned levels of business. It can also use the information to assess the effect of different marketing and promotional strategies. For example, by varying prices and special offers by outlet or region, it can quickly test a new campaign and then introduce it nationally.

If this level of co-operation is to work, it must be mutually beneficial. The retail outlets need to invest time in training staff and managers to make the most effective use of business automation. The local outlet benefits from better local management, simplified ordering, and marketing and promotional campaigns that have been effectively evaluated before they are run nationally. The head-office team gets better control over individual outlets and has better-quality information available to improve the decision-making process.

SUMMARY

This chapter explores the potential for improving business performance when suppliers and local outlets work in partnership. For example, a supplier can provide his own customers with nationwide resources of a consistently high standard, not just by appointing and supporting local outlets, but by working closely with the local outlets to provide the highest standards of service. This section looks at the contribution of both parties to the partnership and also shows how they can use the process to broaden the service they both offer. Partnership can also form the basis for joint ventures that enable both parties to win new business that might not have been feasible without close co-operation. Finally, the chapter looks at the way new communications technology is helping to build stronger business links between suppliers and local outlets.

ACTION CHECKLIST

PARTNERSHIP OPPORTUNITIES

How could you and your local outlets benefit from working more closely together?

Can you use your local outlet's skills and resources to extend your own services?

Can you use partnership to improve control over your local outlets?

What would your local outlets bring you by working more closely with you, and what could you offer them?

What type of opportunities could they exploit by working more closely with you?

What special service could you offer your local outlets in return for greater co-operation?

Can you use partnership to set up loose arrangements for co-operation with other networks?

Can you use your contacts with multinational groups to build business with the group in other territories?

JOINT VENTURES

Can you identify opportunities for joint ventures with local outlets?

What benefits would you expect from the relationship?

Can you use the distributor's local contacts to set up joint presentations to important prospects?

Can you identify local opportunities where you could improve the local outlet's opportunity of winning business?

How would you benefit?

BUSINESS LINKS

How can technology help you to improve relationships with your local outlets?

Can you use information systems to improve control, and to benefit your local outlets?

13

CONTROLLING LOCAL SUPPORT PROGRAMMES

MARKETING BUDGETS

Putting local marketing programmes into operation requires a high degree of planning and co-operation with local outlets; it also requires careful control to ensure that the resources, funds and skills are used effectively. A marketing budget must be carefully allocated so that all outlets enjoy the right level of support and the budget should be tailored to meet local business and marketing objectives.

Establishing budget levels

There are a number of ways of determining budget levels.

- Use the turnover and profit of the outlet as a means of establishing the budget, with each outlet being asked to allocate a percentage of the figure to marketing. The supplier will then allocate a sum that is related to the local outlet's contribution.
- Levy a fixed sum from each outlet as a contribution to a central fund which is used to support national generic programmes. The national levy is probably more appropriate when a company is trying to build an overall brand identity for a network of outlets, but it cannot be so easily tailored to local marketing programmes.
- A combination of the two may be the most appropriate solution if the network contains a large number of smaller outlets which may not have sufficient funds to run effective marketing programmes without central support.

Support options

The budget can be used to provide support in a number of ways:

- to fund the cost of providing local outlets with standard support material or campaigns;
- to fund campaigns originated and run by the outlets;
- to fund the cost of providing kits to local outlets to develop their own support material;
- to support national generic campaigns;
- to fund the cost of staff or agencies that provide professional support and marketing services to local outlets.

Budget coverage

The allocation of the budget and the type of funding will depend on the overall promotional plan. The budget covers the following items:

- maintaining specialist staff to plan, implement and support marketing programmes;
- the cost of any business equipment needed to produce or control marketing support, such as desktop publishing, design workstations, database management systems, in-house design and print services;
- the cost of bought-in marketing services such as research, media buying, design, photography, print, merchandising;
- the production cost of bought-in deliverables such as mail shots, brochures, advertisements, display material, event services;
- the cost of communicating the programmes to local outlets such as programme operating guides, launch guides and programme administration material;
- the cost of managing and controlling the programmes, including financial control, invoicing costs to local outlets, paying professional suppliers, recording and analysing programme performance, reporting internally and to local outlets.

Careful budgeting will produce effective results provided the budget meets the business objectives, but it is too easy simply to give money to local outlets with no real means of measuring the return on investment. While all of the budget items would be appropriate to a campaign run from the head office, the supplier can reduce some of the costs by outsourcing the entire service and appointing an agency to manage the whole programme; this is discussed in more detail later in the section.

CENTRAL MARKETING SUPPORT AND PLANNING

While one of the options available to companies was to provide funds for local outlets to carry out their own marketing operations, this may result in a loss of control and poor, inconsistent results around the network. Central marketing planning and support is therefore a crucial part of the process. The marketing plans and campaigns of each outlet are co-ordinated, and a central unit provides the creative and management services to support the whole programme.

Co-ordinating local advertising

Taking advertising as an example, instead of each outlet buying space or time from local media, the central unit books everything, negotiating with media owners and settling all invoices centrally. The result can be a substantial saving in media costs and a more effective use of the advertising budget.

The central unit might also take responsibility for issuing the advertisement copy to local media – providing advertisements to a consistent standard, meeting insertion dates and ensuring that the advertisements are reproduced to the same high quality throughout the network.

The essential quality of a central unit like this is attention to detail. Local advertisements vary in size, content, presentation, offers and products, and all of these elements can change at short notice to meet tactical marketing requirements. For example, on a priced-offer campaign, the offers are likely to be determined by the local outlet. It provides information to the central unit which incorporates the offers in the local version of a standard advertisement. The central unit arranges to have the advertisement checked by the local outlet before it appears in the press and it needs to have the flexibility to accommodate late changes and still maintain accuracy.

The central unit needs to maintain regular effective contact with the local outlets to ensure they are making the best use of the support programmes available and to help the local outlets to develop the offers that are right for their market. If the advertisements include a response mechanism such as 'send for further information' or 'send for the name of your nearest stockist', the central unit must have the resources to handle and respond quickly to those enquiries.

Advertising resource requirements

A central unit like this should be staffed by someone with experience of managing retail advertising programmes. There is a considerable difference between managing retail advertising programmes and running consumer product campaigns which may have larger budgets but simpler production requirements. As well as a manager, the unit may employ creative and production staff and provide them with the resources they need to produce advertisements. Alternatively, the manager can work with a specialist agency or other supplier to produce the material.

Managing other marketing services

The same techniques and resources can be applied to the management of local direct-marketing programmes; the central unit would be responsible for co-ordinating and managing the local database, using information supplied by the local outlets and would plan and produce direct-mail campaigns, customising them where appropriate with price, product and offer information provided by the outlets.

Resource requirements

The unit would require database management systems and mailing facilities to handle the physical mailing and would also employ staff to write, design and produce mailing items. Alternatively, the manager may work with a specialist direct-marketing company which would produce material to the company's specification.

PROVIDING A BRANCH LITERATURE SERVICE

Publications and merchandising material are an essential element in local support, but the task of ensuring that local outlets are provided with adequate supplies when they need them can be an expensive and time-consuming task.

Assessing requirements

For example, a network with hundreds of different outlets of varying size can present a logistical nightmare to a company that produces a wide range of support material. Each outlet may require different quantities and different combinations of publications, and the problems can multiply when the company is supplying material to an international market with different product and language variations.

Distribution

A planned programme of literature distribution is essential if local outlets are to make the most effective use of their support material. The central unit must co-ordinate the requests for support material from the whole network and co-ordinate these with the overall marketing plan and the supplies of material available. It can then distribute material to the local outlets and arrange billing, if the local outlets are to be charged for their supplies. The literature can either be distributed in a planned way to coincide with marketing campaigns or target stock levels or it can be distributed in response to requests from local outlets.

An efficient ordering and recording system is essential if the system is to operate efficiently. If the literature is tied to a programme launch, the central unit must ensure that all outlets receive their material in time and have clear guidelines on how to use the material.

Guidelines on using literature

Literature can be wasted if it is not used for a specific purpose and each piece of literature should be accompanied by a letter that describes:

- why the literature has been produced;
- who it is aimed at;
- what it contains;
- what results it will achieve;
- when it should be issued;
- what other support material goes with it;
- how to follow it up;
- where to get further supplies.

Wherever possible, local outlets should be encouraged to report on their use of the literature so that the success of the programme can be evaluated. By giving the literature a specific purpose and explaining how it should be used, the central unit can avoid the problem of literature that lies unused in the local outlet or is sent to the wrong prospects. The programme can also be evaluated and measured in the same way as an advertising campaign.

Resource requirements

A central literature operation can be handled in a number of ways:

- using an internal service with a manager and storekeeper, with distribution via the company's own transport services;
- using the storage and distribution services of a printer;
- using a specialist promotional handling service with the facilities to manage, store and distribute material and provide a full reporting and administration service.

PROGRAMME ADMINISTRATION

More complex marketing programmes where local outlets receive rebates for providing specific marketing services need to be administered carefully. For example, an extended warranty programme may require local outlets to provide a repair or replacement service free of charge to customers. The local outlet is then reimbursed by the supplier for the warranty work.

Although this sounds simple in theory, the practical implementation can be extremely complex and can lead to dissatisfaction between customer and local outlet, and between supplier and local outlet. Where an extended warranty is used to attract customers and support local outlets, it should be regarded as a marketing programme and given proper support.

- As a first stage, local outlets should be given a complete guide to operating the warranty programme and a set of documentation that enables them to operate the programme easily and efficiently.
- The supplier's programme administration team should have a thorough understanding of the programme guidelines and should be able to provide the local outlets with any administrative assistance they need.
- Finally, the programme should be simple and quick to administer so that there is minimum delay in handling the administration, reimbursing local outlets or dealing with queries.

The courtesy car programme run by many franchised car dealers involves high levels of administration to ensure that it runs effectively.

- Dealers nominate a group of cars to go on the courtesy car fleet and they obtain a rebate on their original purchase price because of the special use.
- The dealers have to calculate how many vehicles they need and they calculate this using a formula based on the number of service customers they have.
- They claim an allowance based on the number of times these vehicles are used – a unit is earned every time a customer uses a courtesy car and the units are multiplied if the customer keeps the courtesy car overnight or for a longer period than anticipated.
- The dealers have to achieve target levels of courtesy car usage during a quarter to qualify for different levels of rebate and they

also have to change their courtesy car fleet when the vehicles reach a certain age.

A detailed operating guide is issued to all participating dealers to explain the benefits, administrative procedures and operation of the programme. There is also a helpline which dealers can use to get information on any aspect of the programme.

Programmes like this can prove to be unwieldy if they are not managed properly. For example, some of the early courtesy car programmes caused considerable disagreement between manufacturers and dealers because dealers did not understand the basis on which they were paid for use of the vehicles, and this prevented the full use of what was an extremely powerful programme. It is vital that any marketing programme is fully supported by experienced people who understand the dealers' problems and can provide a friendly efficient service.

Resource requirements

If the service is to be run internally, it will need an administrator who can develop and implement the programme guide, a telephone contact specialist to handle dealer queries and a keyboard operator to set up and operate the programme database. Alternatively, the programme can be managed by an agency specialising in programme administration.

SETTING MARKETING STANDARDS

As the book has shown, one of the key requirements of a local marketing development programme is that it promotes consistent standards throughout a network. Marketing programmes can achieve this when they are developed and controlled by the supplier, but marketing programmes originated locally may be harder to control.

Where suppliers are providing funds or material to local outlets to help them develop their own programmes, they should try wherever possible to impose their own marketing standards through a marketing standard guide. The guide sets out the manufacturer's business objectives, its key marketing programmes and its visual standards and this provides clear guidelines for local outlets to integrate their programmes.

USING SUPPORT AGENCIES

Programme administration and control is crucial to the success of marketing support programmes, but it can be time consuming and expensive in terms of resources and skills, and may not represent the best possible return on investment. For this reason, many companies are now using external agencies to manage programmes for them. They pay a fee to the agency and this can be compared with the cost of hiring staff, investing in equipment and the cost of overheads to support an internal team.

The agency provides a complete service, administering the programme and reporting to the manufacturer on programme activity and costs. Provided the agency handles the programme efficiently, it may also save the company further money and release funds for other marketing projects.

Selecting a support agency

Before selecting an agency, the manufacturer needs to set a precise specification for this service so that agencies can provide accurate quotations for comparison. As an example, the specification for a courtesy car programme might include the following requirements:

- provide a comprehensive service to cover the setting up, daily running and administration of the programme and reporting to the manufacturer;
- develop and produce programme documentation;
- provide communications facilities to handle orders, enquiries and problems;
- set up and manage a programme database to record and report on programme activity;

- provide monthly reports on programme activity;
- provide a rebate service to local outlets, with full reporting to the manufacturer.

The specification may be even tighter:

- enrol 200 outlets in the programme;
- set up a dedicated fax and telephone service with three incoming lines to deal with queries;
- respond to local queries within two hours.

The more specific the brief in terms of physical requirements and quality of performance, the better the basis for comparison. The specification for running a local advertising and support service can be specified very precisely:

- produce a guide showing the choice of local advertisements available;
- develop advertisement order forms for local outlets;
- design a set of twelve advertisement formats with variations for eight product offers and a facility for charging prices on each insertion;
- provide three advertisements per month to 200 outlets;
- set up a hotline to handle telephone queries;
- set up a dedicated fax line to receive incoming advertisement orders and fax artwork proofs to local outlets;
- send copy instructions to each publication;
- pay the local outlets a rebate of 50 per cent of media costs;
- produce a quarterly report of programme activity with copies to each of ** sales and marketing staff.

The workload on this programme can be easily quantified. Agencies that handle programme administration can be divided into a number of different categories:

- agencies that are computer based and that handle only administration;
- agencies that come from an accounting background and that handle only administration;
- agencies that specialise in advertising and marketing and that

provide administrative and management services in conjunction with their marketing services;

- agencies that specialise in retail support programmes and that produce an integrated marketing, production and management service.

Programme reporting

Reporting needs to be an integral part of the programme management process to ensure that local outlets are making the most effective use of the marketing programmes and to track and control budget expenditure. On a local advertising support programme, for example, the quarterly report would cover a number of aspects:

- total expenditure on media;
- expenditure by outlet;
- total expenditure to date;
- production costs for the quarter, in total and by outlet.

Reports like this would be available to marketing and sales staff within a company so that they can monitor the activity, analyse it against sales performance and use it to monitor the activity of individual outlets. As part of the reporting procedure, many companies insist on auditing the marketing programmes to ensure that the money is being spent on marketing programmes and that the agency is acting cost effectively.

SUMMARY

This chapter looks at the options for managing and controlling local marketing support. It looks briefly at different budgeting options and examines a number of different approaches to providing central marketing support. Local advertising and other marketing services can be handled centrally for greater efficiency and co-ordination, but the chapter balances this against the resource requirements. It considers the options for providing a branch literature service and explains how guidelines on the use of promotional literature can avoid wasted effort. The chapter looks at different methods of administering and reporting on marketing programmes, emphasising that the most effective administration is often the simplest. It shows how marketing standards can be used to impose consistently high standards on locally-produced material and explains the procedure for selecting and using external support agencies.

ACTION CHECKLIST

BUDGETS

How do you establish your local marketing budget?

Could you improve the effectiveness of your support by budgeting in a different way?

Do all of your outlets contribute to the marketing support programme or do they run their own programmes?

What does your local support budget cover?

Could you handle any of the budget items differently to make more effective use of your budget?

Can you reduce your budget by outsourcing some of the programme management services?

SUPPORT OPTIONS

Are there advantages in handling support centrally?

Is it essential that your marketing activities are completely integrated?

Do you have the resources to co-ordinate a large marketing support programme using your own resources?

Have you compared the real cost of running a central support operation against the cost of an external supplier?

Are your outlets making effective use of your marketing support material?

Could you improve the uptake and use of your support material by communicating its use and benefits to local outlets?

If you use external support agencies, do you have criteria for measuring their effectiveness?

PROGRAMME ADMINISTRATION

Do you provide local outlets with detailed guides to programme administration?

Do you receive a large number of queries about programme administration?

Can you improve the clarity and effectiveness of your programme administration?

CONCLUSION

Local marketing is important to companies supplying a wide variety of products and services in national and international markets. However, the traditional approach of providing uniform support policies means that support may not reflect local market conditions. It is important that local outlets should be treated as independent small businesses, rather than outposts of head office, whether they are franchised outlets, branch offices or independent multi-franchise outlets.

There are a number of success factors that can be used to measure the potential of a local outlet as an independent business, and you can use them to review the current status of your local network and set objectives for improving performance. For example, do your local outlets reflect your long-term business requirements, what are the key tasks in improving performance, and do you have the resources to meet your local marketing objectives? It is, however, essential that you look at marketing support programmes from the point of view of the outlets – what do they want from the relationship with the supplier? Broad market coverage and rapid stock turnover are obvious requirements, but what about the importance of product information, regular contact with local outlets and technical support? Local outlets want backing in the form of training and effective marketing support to build their business and they are keen on participation. By taking the local point of view you will be able to gain commitment to your programmes and attract new outlets of the right calibre.

Research is an essential basis for planning local support, and local knowledge combined with national research data can help to determine the success factors for local marketing and identify the key differentiators that need to be addressed in developing a support package. The planning process must reflect all the important local factors such as key market sectors, competitive activity, customer satisfaction and customer loyalty objectives and skills, and the local marketing plan must reflect the input and interests of both parties.

Effective planning enables you to determine the right level of support for each market and each outlet using a variety of techniques to tailor support programmes to local market conditions. National support programmes are important to meet strategic customer satisfaction and identity objectives, but modular support programmes provide the flexibility to meet the requirements of different markets. Achieving consistent standards is one of the major problems faced by companies marketing through multiple outlets. Consistency enables local outlets to be branded in the same way as products and ensures high levels of customer satisfaction throughout a network. Quality standards such as BS 5750 and targeted training programmes make an important contribution to consistent performance, while performance scatter can be managed by concentrating resources in centres of excellence or by utilising best practice from around their networks. Corporate identity programmes can also help to achieve high standards of visual consistency in diverse networks.

High standards of customer care are essential to building customer satisfaction and loyalty at local level. By researching customers' expectations, customer focus standards can be developed which contribute to consistent standards of customer care in every local outlet. Customer satisfaction is a measurable business process which, when combined with incentive and recognition schemes, can be used to motivate local staff to achieve increasingly higher standards of customer care.

Sales remain a key measure of local performance, and comprehensive information and support can help to build understanding, commitment and increased sales of new and existing products and services. Traditional sales incentives can be structured to meet different marketing objectives, while new technology such as laptop computers and interactive video can be used to develop product knowledge and improve the selling process to the customer. Effective communications help to build understanding and commitment to success at local level. With local outlets placing so much importance on personal contact in national and international markets, a distributor specialist plays a key role in improving communications with local outlets. When suppliers and local outlets work in partnership, the potential for business improvement is enormous. Both parties can broaden the service they offer and win new business through joint ventures.

This book has explained how to improve local marketing performance in a way that benefits both supplier and local outlet. It is an issue of vital importance to senior managers, and perhaps we should conclude with the words of a successful retailer who recognises the importance of the local market – Sir Alastair Grant, Chairman & Chief Executive of Argyll Group Plc:

> *'I have a dream about the future of Safeway. One day we shall have 500 stores, each perfectly adapted to the needs of the community it serves; we shall sell 20,000 products of which a third will be Safeway own brand; these own brands will match or beat the quality of the leading proprietary brands; we shall trade seven days a week and every minute that we are open, we shall fully satisfy every customer.*
>
> *We shall be known and loved by every consumer; known and respected by every supplier; known and admired by every financial institution; known and valued by every member of government; known and understood by every journalist.*
>
> *We are, I judge, about 60 per cent of the way towards my dream. Our marketing reflects both where we are and where we want to be. I apply a marketing point of view to pretty well everything we do and I work at making the idea of marketing pervasive throughout the business.'*

This mission statement sets the direction for everyone in the business. It shows that every manager and every employee is concerned with meeting customer needs, all of the time, whatever they do. Customers – and that, in many ways, includes suppliers, journalists, members of government as well as consumers – tell us 'where we are and where we want to be'; so in managing and planning the future we must always keep the customer in mind. *'We shall have 500 stores each perfectly adapted to the needs of the community it serves'*; we need to be flexible in our approach to our customers and not impose rigid policies that suit our internal requirements. *'Every minute that we are open, we shall fully satisfy every customer'*; that is the ultimate challenge to every manager. It is the reason why the customer must be the focus for every manager.

INDEX